THE RUGBY LEAGUE LIONS

Ray French

THE RUGBY LEAGUE LIONS

AUSTRALIA AND NEW ZEALAND

1984

Sponsored by
Modern Maintenance Products

With an Introduction by
David Oxley, Secretary-general of the Rugby Football League

faber and faber
LONDON · BOSTON

First published in 1985
by Faber and Faber Limited
3 Queen Square London WC1N 3AU

Photoset and printed in Great Britain by
Redwood Burn Ltd Trowbridge Wiltshire
All rights reserved

British Library Cataloguing in Publication Data

French, Ray
The Rugby League Lions: Australia and New
Zealand 1984.
1. Rugby football—Australia   2. Rugby
football—New Zealand
I. Title   II. Modern Maintenance Products
796.33'374   GV945.9.A9

ISBN 0–571–13525–0
ISBN 0–571–13526–9 (pbk)

Contents

Introduction

A Great Britain tour of Australia is one of the toughest assignments a professional player, in any sport, can undertake, and a Rugby League tour is certainly no exception. The pioneer Lions of 1910 and 1914 spent the best part of six months away from home, including long sea voyages in each direction; in Australia, travel was by horse and cart over the most primitive roads. Nevertheless, according to the official brochure for the 1914 tour, the team at least 'would travel out by one of the palatial steamers of the Orient Line'—and, continued the copy-writer, 'the voyage would give welcome rest to our players before commencing their arduous duties and would provide an opportunity of seeing many countries on the way, both interesting and educational'.

However, I doubt if the 1984 Lions were thinking that much about romantic, far-away places, however interesting and educational, when they took off from Heathrow in the middle of May. Humiliated by Australia in 1979 and 1982, and considered fortunate to finish all-square in the 1980 Tests against New Zealand, Britain's international standing had reached its lowest level. The brief for the 1984 Lions was to close the quality gap and to restore pride.

Ray French, widely experienced as player and commentator, and himself a member of Great Britain's 1968 World Cup squad in Australia, is well placed to assess how Britain's youngest-ever Rugby League tourists faced their daunting challenge against the two strongest countries in the world. No previous Lions' tour has been so closely chronicled, so minutely examined. The detail of the tour is all here: the meticulous preparation, the endless miles of travel, accolades in Australia, disappointment in New Zealand, the lessons for the future.

Deeply knowledgeable and perceptive, Ray French has captured the very essence of the tour. I welcome this book as an extremely important addition to Rugby League's growing library and pay tribute, too, to Modern Maintenance Products not only for their generous sponsorship of the tour itself but also for making possible this authoritative publication.

DAVID OXLEY, *Secretary-general, the Rugby Football League*

Acknowledgements

For permission to include photographs the publisher's thanks are due to the following agencies: Christchurch Press Co., Christchurch, New Zealand (25); John Fairfax and Sons, Broadway, Australia (7); *The NZ Herald*, Wilson and Horton, Auckland, New Zealand (23–24, 26–27); *Rugby League Week*, Sydney, Australia (3–6, 11–13, 20–22, 29); Robin Smith, *Rugby League Times*, Auckland, New Zealand (28); and the Andrew Varley Picture Agency (8–10, 14–19, 30).

1

THE MEANING OF TEST RUGBY: GREAT BRITAIN v. AUSTRALIA AND NEW ZEALAND 1906–1958

Racing hearts; excitement overcoming fear as the referee's whistle blows; the explosive start when the passion and fervour of competition deploy the skills that only the best players from each country can provide; the total commitment; the absolute determination to succeed – these have always been the stuff of Rugby League Tests between Britain and Australia and New Zealand. National pride is at stake and no quarter will be given. For eighty minutes spectators will lose themselves in the ebb and flow of physical confrontation, sharing the players' elation at a score or the dismay and disappointment when the opposition takes the lead. The match will be played over again in pubs and clubs for days afterwards, with the efforts of the heroes enthusiastically recounted.

Few other sports can summon the same degree of passion. So why is Rugby League special? Part of the reason is surely the difficulties that have stood in the way of establishing the code. Nowhere were these greater than in New Zealand and Australia in 1906–7. In New Zealand some Rugby Union internationals, notably George Smith, the All Blacks' star wing three-quarter and world-record 440-yards hurdler, and another All Black, Dick Callam, who had seen the fluent, exciting movements and handling opportunities produced by the new Northern Union laws during the successful All Blacks tour of Britain in 1905–6, decided to try to introduce the faster game to New Zealand. Ironically, their plans were given impetus by the shabby treatment the amateur Union players received from their national body when they returned home. It was A. H. Baskerville, a Wellington government official and rugby forward himself, who took up the cudgels on behalf of those players who had lost their jobs or who were otherwise out of pocket as a result of the tour, while the New

Zealand Rugby Union had made a profit of nearly £13,000. And it was Baskerville who became a leading light in the breakaway movement, organizing the first New Zealand tour of Britain in 1907–8.

After he had circularized the Northern Union clubs in England about the possibility of a tour and had received a favourable response, Baskerville set about his task. Operations were furtive, for such was the opposition to payments to players that a leak at that time would have been disastrous. However, within a few months Baskerville had netted four of the All Blacks team of 1905–6 and at least seventeen highly rated provincial players, all prepared to risk their careers in support of Baskerville's bold venture.

The expense of mounting such an ambitious tour was no drawback. The players were so confident of its success that each paid £50 into the accounts to underwrite it. The few who could not afford such a sum were assisted by H. J. Palmer, a Wellington fish merchant who had recently sold his business and who accompanied the party as manager, and by a Mr Gleeson, an Auckland brewer, who was appointed treasurer. A. H. Baskerville, who had organized the tour, officially went as a player. Baskerville's recruiting arrangements were a well kept secret, but a few days before the team sailed the storm broke. A hostile press dubbed the team 'the All Golds' since, as the southern hemisphere's first professionals, their expenses would be paid in the currency of the day, gold sovereigns. Undeterred, they set sail first for Sydney where, by chance, another furore was raging, again arising out of hardship to players.

The principal cause was the insensitive attitude adopted by the Australian Rugby Union, which ignored the plea for financial assistance made by a Sydney player, Alec Burdon, who had lost his job after breaking his collar bone in a match against the All Blacks in 1907, a game which had produced huge receipts from a 41,000 crowd. The injustice of the official attitude led two former professional cricketers, Victor Trumper and 'Sep' Carter, and a local businessman, Jim Giltinan, to promise to pay players about 15 shillings a day when on tour, plus 10 shillings out-of-pocket expenses on normal match days, if a new rugby code could be devised and sides raised to play it.

Not surprisingly, the Australian Union declared that they would outlaw any players who took part in such a venture. But two events conspired to thwart them. First, at the height of the controversy the new professionals arrived in Sydney on their way to Britain, and three matches against a New South Wales team were hastily arranged by Giltinan, who offered about £750 as prize money. Then came the masterstroke. Trumper and Giltinan tempted Herbert Harry ('Dally') Messenger to turn professional. Messenger was a young footballer from Sydney's Double Bay district who had suddenly burst into the headlines with sparkling displays against New Zealand in 1907. Though only 5 feet 7 inches in height, and weighing 12 stone 7 pounds, this grandson of a one-

1. The legendary Dally Messenger. Though only 5 feet 7 inches in height and weighing 12 stone 7 pounds, Messenger was a brilliant, unorthodox player, the first Australian Rugby League star.

time champion sculler of England was a brilliant player, unconventional even to the extent of causing a law change. Playing in one match, he used the ploy of throwing the ball forward over a would-be tackler's head and doubling round to gather before it touched the ground. 'A man shoots through from the others,' wrote a commentator at the time, 'fields the ball at top pace, darts off straight, then turns like a hare when blocked and cuts clean away from the defence. That man is Messenger.'

The hero of the Australian crowds did not find the offer to turn professional hard to resist, as he was given £200 for the three matches while the rest of the rebel squad had to be content with £1 10 shillings for each match. But it was a shrewd investment, for as Harry Sunderland, the famous Australian administrator and broadcaster once said, 'Without Messenger's magical appeal at a time when Union was at its strongest in the eastern states, there would have been no Rugby League in Australia today.'

Ironically, because neither the New Zealanders nor the Australians at this stage had much idea of the laws of the breakaway code, they played with fifteen men a side. But following the three demonstration matches, all won by the New Zealanders, despite Messenger's brilliance, it was decided to adopt the thirteen-a-side game. In fact, the decision rested on the casting vote of chairman Harry Hoyle, at a meeting at Bateman's Hotel, George Street, Sydney. Had the vote gone the other way, it could so easily have led to professional Rugby Union instead. Giltinan and Trumper now turned their attention to creating eight new clubs – North Sydney, Glebe, South Sydney, Balmain, Newtown, Eastern Suburbs, Cumberland and a team from Newcastle – for the start of the first Rugby League season in Australia.

In the meantime Baskerville, with his New Zealanders, had arrived in Britain for the first ever international Rugby League tour. He had signed up Messenger, who was to become the star of the tour, scoring 145 points and helping the tourists to win nineteen of the thirty-five matches played. The tour marked the true beginnings of New Zealand Rugby League and was crowned by the team's 2–1 victory in the Test series, though they had not seen a copy of the laws until they arrived in England and had had only nine days before the first match in which to practise them. Adaptable men! However, Baskerville's organization was so good, and so confident was he of financial success, that after a promising 15,000 crowd had watched their match against Wales at the Athletic Ground, Aberdare, on 1 January 1908, he decided to order high tea for all the party at the Boot Hotel at a cost of 3s. 6d. a head. The tour made well over £5,000 profit, and Baskerville was able to pay each of those early pioneers a bonus of £220 per man, a huge sum in those days.

The tour also gave the code in Britain a boost, with players such as Turtill, Smith, McGregor, Wrigley and Todd staying on to enhance the game in this country. Lance Todd later became a leading manager with Salford and gave his name to the individual trophy awarded to the man of the match after the Challenge Cup final at Wembley.

Baskerville, however, had not finished yet, for this remarkable man took his side back to Australia to start Test match rugby there. He also planted the seeds of the Australian tour to Britain in 1908–9. Unfortunately, that Australian tour was not a playing success, nor was it profitable. But its implications for Rugby League should not be underestimated. The Australians overcame great problems and proved worthy ambassadors of Australian sport, and in the wake of the New Zealanders they cemented excellent relations with the Northern Union in Britain.

Though Rugby League in Britain has been confined to Lancashire, Yorkshire and Cumbria for most of its history, and despite the failure of sporadic attempts to spread the game nationally before the welcome appearance of such southern clubs as Fulham, Cardiff (now Bridgend) and Kent Invicta (now Southend Invicta), there has always been a specially intense patriotic pride in playing a Test match. Indeed, the fact that they come from a relatively small geographical area is, I believe, a major reason why British players and administrators have retained this special pride in country and team.

When, in 1910, the first British tourists to Australia steamed out of Tilbury on the Orient liner *Osterley*, under the leadership of the Cumbrian centre, James Lomas, wearing their straw hats complete with tour badge – the only clothing they had been issued with, so most had to wear their Sunday suits – few realized they would return with the Ashes and a bonus of £30 each gained from the 40,000 crowds that were to watch their games in Sydney. Those players, men like Billy Batten (the great Hunslet and Hull wing) and James Leytham (of Wigan), a leading points scorer in his day, were to display tremendous physical courage and an absolute determination to win that would make memorable many Britain v. Australia Tests in the years to come. It is worth recalling three of the most famous of them – the 'Rorke's Drift' Test (named after the Zulu battle) of 1914, the first Test of the 1948 series at Headingley, and the second Test in Brisbane in 1958, each of them an heroic contest.

Third Test, Australia v. Great Britain
(The 'Rorke's Drift' Test)
Sydney, 4 July 1914
Australia 6   Great Britain 14

The 1914 tour party arrived in Australia at a time when Rugby League, after only seven years had emerged as the more popular of the two rugby codes in the states of New South Wales and Queensland. The fortunes of the tour were in the hands of two experienced managers, Joe Houghton (St Helens) and John Clifford (Huddersfield), while the captaincy had been entrusted to the 'prince of centres', Harold Wagstaff of Huddersfield. Though only 22 years old, the ex-Underbank junior had gained every honour possible in the game and was acclaimed 'a master at drawing his man and timing his pass'. The word 'dignity' is frequently attached to his name in the early records, and he was certainly able to claim that accolade after the trials and tribulations which he had to endure on that tour.

In typical vitriolic style, the Australian press, following defeats for Britain in their first two matches in Sydney, declared that the British team would be better matched against 'a team of College girls'. Casting aside such criticism, Wagstaff's side thrashed the Kangaroos in the first Test 23–5, but the second Test was played only two days later, on the Monday, the King's birthday, when Great Britain, now lacking such star players as Jarman, Longstaff, Moorhouse and Jenkins, were hard pressed to raise a team. Not surprisingly, they were beaten by 12–7 and the battle for the Ashes stood square.

It was at this stage, however, that politics entered the fray, causing further problems for skipper Wagstaff, as he himself readily admitted:

> 'The arrangement was that the final Test would be played in Melbourne when we returned from New Zealand. An England v. New South Wales game was fixed for Sydney the following Saturday and, on the Wednesday morning, Mr Clifford, one of our managers, took a team to Bathurst. Then the Australians began an agitation for the third Test to be played in place of the New South Wales match. Mr Clifford could not be consulted and eventually the Australian authorities cabled to England to ask the Northern Union council to agree to the third Test being played as the Australians wished.
>
> A special meeting of the Northern Union council was called. They agreed to the Australian demand and sent the following message to the British party in Australia: 'Play match as Australians desire. England expects that every man will do his duty.' So it came about that the third Test was played on the Saturday following the first – three Tests in eight days for a touring team crippled by injury!'

The mood, not unnaturally, was a sombre one as the British party kept to its hotel on the evening before the deciding match but, such is the spirit engendered on such tours, the outlook changed rapidly thanks to the antics of the star forward Douglas Clark. Clark had bought a 6-foot snake during the day and had hidden it in a cardboard box. When he released the reptile in the hotel corridors panic set in as guests barricaded their doors and the hotel management set about catching it. They caught the snake, but not before it had crept inside Walt Guerin's pyjamas and wrapped itself round his waist in an ever-tightening grip. The grip was duly relaxed, the snake placed back in its box and sanity was restored. But Clark had lifted the depression and, despite the fright, the players were laughing again next morning.

The laughing had stopped, however, when Australia ran on to the Sydney Cricket Ground that afternoon to the tune of 'See the Conquering Hero Comes', the strains of which could be heard faintly below the incessant chants of the crowd, 'Blues, Blues' (then the colour of the Australian shirts). Harold Wagstaff himself best illustrates the dramatic events of that day:

'My first memory of the day in which the match was played has to do with the fighting speech that was made to us by Mr Clifford. He called the men who were playing that afternoon – the thirteen of us – into a room at the hotel and he outlined the whole story of the revision of the fixtures. Then he said that he expected every one of us to play as we had never played before. 'You are playing in a game of football this afternoon but more than that you're playing for England. Don't forget the message from home: England expects every one of you to do his duty.'

The men in my team were moved. I was impressed and thrilled as never before or since by a speech. You could see our fellows clenching their fists as Mr Clifford spoke, and I know that when he left that room none of us spoke.

We were prepared to go all out when we went on to that field in Sydney, but, before there had been a scrum, Frank Williams, on the wing, had twisted his leg. We took 'Chick' Johnson out of the pack to help Williams on that wing. We managed to lead 9–3 at half time. Percy Coldrick had scored a try and Alf Wood had kicked three goals. Immediately we started the second half Douglas Clark smashed his collar bone. He had broken a thumb in the first half and it had been bandaged tightly so that he could continue. In the early stages of the second half Clark got a pass and went racing clear of all, it seemed, for the line, but Pony Halloway challenged him. Douglas started to hand off Halloway and then remembered his broken thumb. He withdrew the hand and went into Halloway to give him his shoulder, but Halloway stalled and Clark, unable to recover his balance, fell on his shoulder and the collar bone went. He had it strapped and twice made an effort to return to the game, but in the end realized that it was impossible to carry on. There were tears in his eyes when he left the field for the last time.

Frank Williams hurt his leg again and he had to go off, and we were left with eleven men. Then Billy Hall of Oldham was carried off with concussion – and we had ten men to face thirteen. Ten men and thirty minutes to go! But never had I nine such men with me on a football field as I had that day. We were in our own half all the time, and for most of it we seemed to be on our own line, but we stuck it. Our forwards gave their all. In the scrummages the remnants of the pack did their job, and in the loose the men who had been brought out of the pack tackled as fiercely and as finely as the backs: Chick Johnson on one wing and Coldrick on the other, and Willie Davies in the centre with me.

17

As often happens in such circumstances, we continued to win the ball from the scrums. Holland, Ramsdale and Chilcott were heroes. There were twenty minutes left when I managed to cut through after taking the ball from Fred Smith and Prosser. I went to Johnson's wing and, when I gave Chick the ball, there was only the full-back in front of him. Chick went away with it, but then none of us dreamed that we were to witness the scoring of as wonderful a try as Test football will produce. A few yards from the Australian full-back he put the ball on the ground and began to dribble. He had half the length of the field to go, but he did it. And the ball never left his toes. It might have been tied with a piece of string to his feet, so perfectly did he control it. No soccer international could have dribbled a ball better than did Johnson that afternoon on Sydney Cricket Ground. Man after man he beat until, finally, he tapped the ball over the line and dropped on it. Alf Wood kicked the goal, and there we were, 14–3. Billy Hall recovered and came back for the last ten minutes to help us in defence that was successful until, in the last few minutes, Sid Deane scored Australia's second try.

But the victory was ours and the Australian crowd gave us full credit for it. They swung round to our side in the second half, and they were with us to the end, cheering us on in inspiring fashion. When the whistle sounded we were done. We had gone to the last gasp and were just about finished.'

The tactic used by Chick Johnson in scoring the winning try may seem a strange one to the modern spectator, but he knew what he was doing. It was not for nothing that he was called 'the greatest dribbler in the Northern Union', for his speciality, as in the style of the old Rugby Union forwards, was to break away from a scrum and wheel out with the ball at his feet. Such a tactic meant that he could control the ball skilfully while none of the Australian defenders could tackle him and thus stop his movement forward. This Widnes policeman used his brains as well as his feet!

Great Britain: Wood (Oldham); Williams (Halifax), Hall (Oldham), Wagstaff (Huddersfield), captain, Davies (Leeds); Smith (Hunslet), Prosser (Halifax); Holland (Oldham), Coldrick (Wigan), Ramsdale (Wigan), Johnson (Widnes), Clark (Huddersfield), Chilcott (Huddersfield)

Australia: Hallett; Frawley, Deane, captain, Tidyman, W. Messenger; Fraser, Halloway; Burge, Courtney, Craig, Sullivan, Pearce, Cann

First Test, Great Britain v. Australia
Headingley, Leeds, 9 October 1948
Great Britain 23   Australia 21

Before the Second World War Great Britain had led the way in the traditional skills of the game, and the first series at home in peacetime in 1948 gave ample indication that Britain intended to maintain that dominance. This was to continue for a further fifteen years until Britain's adversaries, by superior coaching and organization, coupled with greater individual player motivation, began to develop those very skills and to learn those very lessons which were rammed home so effectively under Ernest Ward's captaincy against the Australians in 1948.

'The match will long live in the memories of those who were privileged to see it. I am equally sure it will live in the minds of the twenty-six players who took part,' wrote Eddie Waring at the time, giving the first Test at Headingley, Leeds, on 9 October 1948, the highest praise. That match, and the quality of play throughout the tour, certainly deserved such an accolade. The 36,000 spectators who thronged the ground witnessed a truly remarkable game blending outstanding individual skills with the highest standards of physical fitness.

The Kangaroos' team had in Clive Churchill the best Australian full-back of the post-war years. Though only 5 feet 7 inches in height and weighing 11 stone 10 pounds, he was a deadly tackler who had a habit of chopping players down at the knees. He had the sheer pace to time a tackle and also to link up in attack, find the gap, and leave defenders trailing with his electrifying bursts. Wally O'Connell, at stand-off, was a hard, nuggety type rather in the mould of Cec Mountford, the great New Zealand and Wigan player, while Doug McRitchie, at 13 stone 6 pounds, was 'strong and afraid of nothing', in the opinion of his opposite centre Albert Pimblett. 'We always knew he was there. It was a hospital job if you didn't watch him in the tackle.' The forwards were physical and aggressive, and yet it was the blend of skills of the Great Britain side which triumphed. As Pimblett concludes: 'We had far more ability; they were just rugged players – no set moves, and straightforward runners. We had the edge in pace and fitness. I was on a winning side five times against them that season. Got sick of beating them.' Such was the confidence!

Meeting on the Wednesday prior to the match at the Griffin Hotel, Leeds, the players first watched the Australians play at Castleford in the evening to assess their strengths and weaknesses before training themselves on the

Thursday and Friday. 'We talked together, worked out moves together and practised under captain Ernest Ward. No one was directing us. This was good sense on Ernie's part, for he merely adopted the moves that Helme and I used at Warrington and everybody chipped in with their ideas. Egan put the forwards through their drills.' As Pimblett indicates, such reliance on the players' individual skills enabled them to express their talents naturally, and fitness levels were entirely the responsibility of the individual. Here again we should note, especially in the case of Albert Pimblett who had suffered such serious wounds in his back in the war that he feared he might never play again, the courage, determination and pride that would bring each member of the squad back for extra training night after night. 'We spent hours on the cinder track at Ruskin Park, St Helens, in extra training three and four days a week and then paid old Joe Carson 2s. 6d. for a rub down,' Pimblett would recall.

Stan McCormick, a player in that series and later a coach with St Helens and Salford, remembers his days on the track with affection, 'It was your own personal pride which made you do it.' Such was their success in winning that Test series 3–0 that one local commentator could say, 'The old cry for a coach for the Great Britain team has now faded away. No coach could have achieved more – probably he would not have achieved as much as the system they adopted. Players were allowed to develop their own ideas and, within their limitations, to play accordingly.'

Twelve tries, seven to Great Britain and five to Australia, indicate the sway and excitement of the match, as Australia took a 6-points lead after only twenty minutes, with tries from Hall and McMahon. By half-time Great Britain were back in control at 11–6 through two tries by Foster and one from McCormick, who left Churchill 'for dead' after a glorious sidestep. Ernest Ward tacked on his side's solitary goal of the afternoon. Pimblett's pace, developed during his youth athletic days, caused havoc in the Kangaroo defence as he raced in for two more tries. Another try-scoring run from McCormick and one from loose-forward Valentine were enough, despite the Kangaroos' late rally, to make the score 23–21 in Britain's favour with five minutes to go. Skills performed at speed were the bases of success, for with only the two centres, weighing more than 13 stone, and the other five in the back division only averaging 11 stone 4 pounds, there was little else they could rely on behind the scrum.

As in every era of Test rugby, the laws dictate the style of play and here, at a time when sixty or seventy scrums were common, the front row of Gee, Egan and Curran maintained possession nearly all the time. Such an amount of scrummaging kept the forwards in the middle of the field, where more often than not they were used simply to clear the ball away from their own 25-yard area, releasing it, only too gratefully, to the backs.

2.   Whether in a Test match or just a tour game, competition between Britain and Australia has always been keen, the desire to win uppermost. How often have we seen incidents like this, in the St Helens v Australia match at Knowsley Road on 27 September 1952? Will Stan McCormick, the St Helens and Great Britain wing, outpace the covering Australian centre Hazzard? There is nothing but total commitment in the faces of both players.

'You can't run 60 yards and scrum and forage properly at the same time,' was the comment of the mighty Wigan prop, Ken Gee. But the backs could, and they revelled in the wider spaces, using close-forward play only when the occasion demanded it, as in the last five minutes of the match. Then, using the unlimited tackle rule to its full advantage, the pack retained possession of the ball in a series of forward charges, another example of skills and physique being harnessed for the tactical exploitation of the laws of the time.

Great Britain: Ledgard (Leigh); Lawrenson (Wigan), Ward (Bradford Northern), captain, Pimblett (Warrington), McCormick (Belle Vue Rangers); Horne (Barrow), Helme (Warrington); Gee (Wigan), Egan (Wigan), Curran (Salford), Nicholson (Huddersfield), Foster (Bradford Northern), Valentine (Huddersfield)

Australia: Churchill; McMahon, McRitchie, Hawke, Graves; O'Connell, captain, Froome; Gibbs, Schubert, Holland, Hall, Rayner, Mulligan

---

Second Test, Australia v. Great Britain
Brisbane, 5 July 1958
Australia 18   Great Britain 25

Alan Prescott's Lions' side of 1958 has been rated one of the best ever to tour Australia and New Zealand, losing only one match out of twenty-one in the Australian section of the trip. The team had set off at a whirlwind pace by winning six of their first seven matches, but had stumbled badly in the first Test, losing 8–25 before a huge crowd of 68,777 in Sydney. As a result the management team of Barney Manson and the genial Tom Mitchell had to endure considerable criticism with regard to team selection, while coach Jim Brough also came in for some rough treatment. The team clearly needed steadying, and it was a shrewd move to take them to Surfers Paradise, near Brisbane, for training. This was just the tonic they needed. Even so, few could have foreseen the dramatic events that were to follow.

Soon after the start of the match Prescott, the captain, received an injury to his right arm. But he felt he could wait until half-time for treatment, so he gamely struggled on, gritting his teeth at the pain as he made contact at every scrum with his opposite front row. Shortly afterwards, stand-off Bolton broke his shoulder and had to be taken from the field, leaving Britain with twelve men, there being no substitute rule at that time. Despite these problems the Lions were the superior side and led 10–2 at half-time when Prescott's arm was to be looked at.

As is usual in a Rugby League dressing-room at half-time, many players were demanding plasters, tape and scissors as they attended to cuts and bruises. Suddenly the hubbub was shattered when the Australian doctor announced that Prescott had broken his arm and could take no further part in the game. There were long seconds of total silence. How could Great Britain win with eleven men? Prescott, however, had other ideas and, much to the doctor's consternation, announced that he would continue, insisting that Australia were not to know the extent of his injury. And in an attempt to put a defensive clamp on the attacking skills of the Aussies, it was agreed that Karalius, the loose forward, would keep out from the pack at stand-off. Prescott, though unable to use his broken arm, still did his stint of tackling – as he said, 'making green and gold shirts either go over me or round me'. He still ran with the ball, holding it tucked into his chest with his left arm, and helped to relieve pressure when on his own line. His display of courage and pride became infectious, for despite a late flurry of points for Australia, Great Britain sealed a famous victory 25–18. Prescott's inspirational leadership continued to be felt in the third Test, and his team (minus himself) brought off a convincing 40–17 victory in that game too.

Great Britain: Fraser (Warrington); Southward (Workington Town), Ashton (Wigan), Challinor (Warrington), Sullivan (Wigan); Bolton (Wigan), Murphy (St Helens); Prescott (St Helens), captain, Harris (Hull), McTigue (Wigan), Huddart (Whitehaven), Whiteley (Hull), Karalius (St Helens)

Australia: Clifford; Diamond, Carlson, Hawick, Kite; Brown, Holman; Davies, Kearney, Marsh, Mossop, Provan, O'Shea

Of course, such matches as the 'Rorke's Drift' Test and Alan Prescott's epic battle in Brisbane were played under rules different from those of today: the number of scrums was far greater, and the number of tackles after which the ball could be retained was unlimited. Thus it was possible for a weaker team, even down to ten men, to take on a side of full strength, keeping the ball for long stretches through committed scrummaging and the eradication of mistakes when in possession. This is almost impossible in the modern game where the ball, because of the six-tackle rule, passes rapidly from team to team. Nevertheless, these three matches were won principally through displays of extraordinary courage, pride and total commitment. The heroics of Wagstaff's team in 1914 were still to be seen at Headingley in 1948 and ten years later in the shape of the gallant Alan Prescott as he led his side to that spectacular victory in Brisbane.

2

RUGBY LEAGUE IN AUSTRALIA

The question most frequently asked by the thousands of spectators who watched the rout of Great Britain by Australia in the 1982 Test series was who could possibly provide competitive opposition for the Kangaroos in the years ahead? As the Australian side swept to fifteen victories in Britain, scoring some ninety-seven tries, with only seven tries against, the 181,000 spectators who watched them enthused over the quality of their play. They became one of the great sporting attractions of any era, admired for their skills and athleticism, in particular by the rival Rugby Union code which also recognized the Australians' impregnable position in world rugby.

Norman Harris of the *Sunday Times* was prompted to write: 'Who would have thought that a team from Rugby League would provide a lesson which promises to be the most profound ever experienced by Rugby Union football?' Dick Greenwood, the coach to the England Rugby Union side, was even more forthright when he concluded that 'videos of the three Rugby League Tests should be compulsory viewing for every serious Rugby Union player.'

Dick Greenwood's assertion was right, not only for his Union players but for all who had Rugby League's interests at heart, whether player, administrator or spectator. International Test matches are a barometer of the health of any sport, and the 1982 series reflected the ailing condition of Rugby League in Britain and the well-being of the game in Australia. The public's mood changed rapidly as they watched the three Tests, only to become aware, at the end of the series, of the wide gulf in ability between the two teams and, in particular, the differences in structure and standards between the two competing nations.

A sense of outrage and shock was the first reaction to Great Britain's 4–40 drubbing at the hands of the Kangaroos in the first Test at Hull. The many thousands who were locked out of the ground at Boothferry Park missed an exhibition of Rugby League skills not seen for years in Britain. Though the half-time score was only 10–4 in the Australians' favour, the crowd had already seen their highly efficient tackling and defensive strategy, sharpened by hours of drills and practices, which would prevent any side from defeating them. In the second half the spectators saw a bewildering display of high-speed running, precision passing and expertly worked moves which were to produce five further tries. The try by the second-row forward, Wayne Pearce, in the twenty-fourth minute of the second half, when he and fellow forward Craig Young outpaced the entire Great Britain cover over 70 yards, amply illustrated the differences in fitness and speed. The crowd was shocked; the general public blamed the coaches, John Whiteley and Colin Hutton; the press lambasted the tackling of the British side, and their readers wrote letters to every conceivable newspaper and magazine, attributing Britain's downfall to that old bogey 'selection'. The differences in skill between the two nations and the inadequacies of the structure of the Rugby Football League were not then fully understood: realization was to come during and after the second Test at Wigan on 20 November 1982.

It was only after three weeks of soul searching, prompted mainly by the media, that the fans acknowledged the gulf in approach and class of the tourists. And their appreciation was seen during the second Test when, although Britain lost 6–27 and were at the receiving end of a five-try blitz, the whole of the Wigan crowd applauded spontaneously as the ball was passed at speed through twelve pairs of Australian hands in one continuous movement without a British player being able to make a tackle. At that moment in the second half, when Krilich, Lewis, Sterling, Rogers, Boustead, Sterling (again), Reddy, Pearce, Lewis, Kenny, Lewis (again) and Price displayed their running and handling skills, the British public recovered from their humiliation and could at last appreciate the status of Australian Rugby League. As Paul Fitzpatrick observed in his summing up of that particular movement in his *Rugby League Review 1982–83*: 'There was no try to celebrate at the end of it, but rarely in sport can a team have won such ungrudging admiration from their opponents' supporters as Australia received then.' A week later, on Sunday, 28 November, the spectators had more to admire during the third Test at Headingley, Leeds. Despite a gallant effort by Britain in restricting the Australians to a 14–8 lead with ten minutes to go, and despite Steve Evans (Hull) scoring their first try of the series, the fans applauded enthusiastically and even urged the time-keeper to restrain his hooter as the Kangaroos swept in four more tries. Boustead, Rogers, Pearce and finally Kenny all crossed the line with, for the first time in my experience, the home crowd urging them on. At the end of the match they invaded the pitch to cheer skipper Max Krilich when he was presented with the Ashes Trophy. It was a spontaneous tribute to a winning team who had played vintage rugby. Such respect for true champions is accorded only rarely in Rugby League. The last occasion was in 1958, when the fair-minded Sydney public applauded Alan Prescott, his arm in a plaster cast, and his gallant Ashes-winning team as they paraded around the Sydney Cricket Ground.

Though the skills of players like Meninga, Sterling, Rogers, Pearce and Price were admired throughout the country, it was the application and thinking of the coach behind the players that harnessed their talents on the field. A product of the coaching network set up in the early 1960s in Australia, coach Frank Stanton's success was the fruit of all the hard work and ideas that had gone into establishing Australia's National Coaching Scheme. In fact, all the modern thinking adapted from American grid-iron football, athletics and Australian Rules football, the psychoanalysis of players and the use of modern aids, such as video cassettes and tape recorders, and new equipment like tackling shields and punch bags, did no more than revive the old virtues of outstanding physical courage allied to playing skills and an absolute determination to succeed that are necessary for victory at Test level. In any event, in 1982 Frank Stanton was rightly regarded as the finest Rugby League coach in the world simply because he, above all others, had rediscovered what was required for Test victory and was prepared to adopt the new techniques to achieve it.

But success also depends on playing to the current laws of the game, and Stanton was shrewd enough to realize that he needed fitness and speed in his team, if they were to cope with the demands of the six-tackle rule. This limit on the number of times a team can be tackled while still maintaining possession of the ball cries out for fitter and faster forwards and requires that teams should be able to play a more open and free-flowing game. Complacency then reigned over this rule in Britain, and coaches paid only lip-service to its demands.

There is no doubt that in 1982 the Australian League player was fitter and more dedicated than his counterpart in Britain, and that far higher standards of fitness were demanded by Australian clubs. Few teams in Britain were carrying out intensive four and five training sessions a week as the major Sydney clubs were, and few British internationals were working to the rigorous fitness tests to which even average players were subjected in Australia. What was lacking was the dedication and application required to carry out individual training schedules parallel to those of the club. Consequently, Frank Stanton's players were attuned to his punishing schedules when on tour and accustomed to the invigorating ideas on speedwork which he absorbed from other sports. As with second-row forward Wayne Pearce, who regularly went on daily runs by himself and always finished his training by running up the stairs to his room at the Dragonara Hotel, Leeds, the players looked after their own individual fitness outside the daily organized sessions.

Stanton's psychoanalysis of all his players prior to the tour gave him a better idea of each player's personality; the careful analysis of who roomed with whom, the introvert with the extrovert, aided team unity. His insistence on weekly meetings behind locked doors, with only the players and himself present, excluding even the managers, allowed the players to criticize or praise all aspects of play as well as the organization of the tour. Players' performances were openly discussed; strengths and weaknesses were thrashed out in private. Such tactics were unknown to the British, yet all Frank Stanton was doing was developing a team spirit and confidence in each other's abilities that, prior to the days of coaches, captains like Harold Wagstaff and Ernest Ward created in discussions with their players on the field.

I remember, from one of my trips to Leeds to watch the Australians in training before the first Test, how quiet yet effective Stanton was as he moved about the field. Experienced players like Reddy, Price, Rogers and Krilich, not Stanton, took the groups in training. They issued the orders and chided the others when things were a little slack. Younger players like Pearce and Sterling were later given charge of various skill practices, thereby increasing their confidence and bringing them more to the front in the tour party. Stanton was never dictatorial. But, as with the great tour captains of the past, while he let players express themselves in training sessions, he made sure that his own demands were met.

When the Great Britain wing, Stan McCormick, remarked how pride in the Great Britain shirt inspired the players in the 1948 series, and when that pride was expressed through the extraordinary courage of the injured Alan Prescott in 1958, both players were highlighting another factor in Stanton's success. Stanton motivated his team by playing strong, stirring tunes like 'The Fighting Kangaroos' or 'The Eye of the Tiger' in the coach on the way to matches. He showed video recordings of brilliant moves by his own players back home in Australia, and for 'anti-Pommie' effect he used a clip of Botham's innings in England's cricket Ashes victory of 1981. These and many other technical aids used on the tour helped to give his players supreme confidence and, above all, pride in their Australian green and gold jersey. Yet I feel sure that Stanton would be the first to acknowledge that he and his team simply stood at the top of a pyramid that was based on the solid structure of Australian Rugby League at all levels.

In 1964 Peter Corcoran, the Australian director of coaching, having studied the coaching methods of many other sports and especially grid-iron football in America, related all these ideas to Rugby League. A coaching manual was produced and coaching courses were initiated. This coaching scheme was supported by the Australian Rugby League and had the wholehearted backing of the major Sydney clubs, which ensured that only those who became qualified coaches could be engaged by professional clubs. Such a lead from the professional side of the game meant that amateur clubs and schools and youth organizations were quick to adopt the scheme. Soon the right men with the correct coaching techniques were at work, and with a vast schools and youth network in Australia to draw on, it has not taken long to produce quality players.

An idea of the immense size of junior Rugby League can be gauged from the fact that in the 1982 season, in just one team area of Sydney, Parramatta, there were thirty-five leagues flourishing from Under-18s down to Under-7s, catering for 353 teams with well over 5,000 registered youngsters. In addition, there is a sizeable schools network, especially in New South Wales, where the long-standing and prestigious University Shield and Buckley Shield for Under-18 and Under-14 levels attract almost 500 teams. The competition for the NSW Combined High Schools is sponsored by the Commonwealth Bank to the extent of A$25,000 per season and frequently attracts television coverage for its final. Similar youth and schools organizations flourish in the other major League playing state, Queensland, while there have been recent developments also in Western Australia, Victoria and the Northern Territory, areas long neglected by the once fiercely parochial Sydney administration.

Obviously, to maintain such a vast youth structure a lot of money has to be generated by the major professional clubs in Sydney, clubs like St George, South Sydney and Eastern Suburbs. These are financed by a network of satellite social clubs, with many thousands of members, and are equipped with swimming pools, restaurants, bars, cabarets, snooker parlours, discos, saunas and so on and, above all, with the one-armed-bandit machines to which most Australians seem addicted. Some clubs have over 500 of these poker machines, and it is not unusual for one of the Sydney clubs to return $1 million profit a year on them.

One-armed-bandits, however, are banned in Queensland, so there Rugby League clubs have had to learn to be self-sufficient; the clubs obtain their extra revenue from sponsorship, bar profits and fund-raising ventures. Clubs in north and central Queensland, such as Cairns, Townsville, Rockhampton and Mount Isa, are financed, in all essentials, like the larger Union clubs in Britain; but the Brisbane League, comprising eight clubs – Easts, Souths, Valleys, Redcliffe, Wynnum-Manly, Brothers, Wests and Norths – is highly professional and competitive. Indeed, the more conservative financial structure of the Brisbane clubs has enabled them to face the present harsh economic climate much better than many of their Sydney counterparts, too used to vast hand-outs from their associated clubs.

There is little doubt that the three most important factors in the development of Australian Rugby League to its peak in the Test series of 1982 were its National Coaching Scheme, the important financial assistance provided by sponsorship, the network of satellite clubs and so on, and the considerable

3.   Always in the thick of it and leading by example, the Lions' captain and hooker Brian Noble wins an untidy scrum in the match against North Coast at Wauchope on 25 May. His contorted body protects the heel as Neil Holding ferrets for the ball, quickly checking which player is at hand to pass to.

media coverage which is always pushing the game to the front of the public's mind. Ironically, it is the last two factors that are now threatening the game, particularly in Sydney. The over-exposure of Rugby League in the media, especially by the various television channels, has caused a significant drop in attendances from the early 1960s, when 2 million spectators watched a season's games in Sydney. As with soccer in Britain, such over-exposure of recorded highlights, match analyses and interviews has given rise to too many armchair

29

spectators. Television can be of tremendous service to a sport, but there is a point where saturation coverage can be detrimental. And that point, many would argue, has long been reached in Sydney, where at the weekend one can watch televised League literally from morning till night.

Television, however, cannot be blamed for everything; the somewhat stereotyped nature of the play in ordinary League matches, especially in Sydney, has also contributed to the drop in attendances. Though fitness standards have been raised and emphasis placed on strength and speed, League games have become defence-orientated. All teams in Sydney base their game on strong defensive patterns, and their players perform like tackling robots. Hence, with defence seen as the criterion for success, many of the games have become battles of attrition, as teams of equally fit and motivated players are locked in trials of strength. While watching a number of Sydney club matches in 1981 and 1984, I must confess to being bored by the lack of individuality and flair as teams cancelled each other out.

However, the major problem facing the once seemingly impregnable Sydney clubs is that of finance. Though attendances over the past fifteen years have been falling, Rugby League managers have always known that they would get the cash they needed from their associated social clubs. But in the last couple of seasons, recession and the introduction of random breath tests for drunken driving have brought about a sharp drop in attendance at the social clubs and a corresponding decline in the number of people playing the poker machines. The spiral continues with a huge drop in income for the rugby clubs. Reduced income has spelled disaster for those who have wasted their resources by paying out high wages to star players on contracts signed in less stringent times. Some clubs have had to face the fact that their very existence is now threatened.

The system of players' contracts itself has also been the cause of trouble. Unlike the British system, a player's contract in Australia until recently entitled him to leave a club at the end of his term of contract without the club being paid any transfer fee. The player could negotiate a new contract either with his present club or with a new club. Such a contract system, legally enforced after the Dennis Tutty (Balmain) court case in 1967 when Tutty pleaded for, and won, the right to freedom of contract, was a disaster for clubs like Western Suburbs and Newtown. Such clubs, famous for producing a nursery of young stars, have seen players snatched away to the higher placed and bigger fee-paying clubs without any compensation. Over thirty-two players alone have been enticed from Western Suburbs in the last five years. Now, thankfully, a system of transfer fees and compensation is again in force.

Sadly, the new contracts system has come too late for some. The 1983 season almost saw the collapse of two once-famous clubs – Western Suburbs, one of the founder members of the Australian Rugby League in 1908, and Newtown – both of them suffering severe financial deficits. On 26 September 1983 the forty-six-man New South Wales general committee, after a two-and-a-half-hour debate, voted not to invite the two teams to compete in the 1984 season. The committee virtually dealt a death blow to the Western Suburbs club and provided a severe setback to Newtown, who now hope to re-emerge in 1985 or 1986 by amalgamating with a club in the Campbelltown area. Western Suburbs, however, were later able to restore their ailing finances, rejoined the Sydney League for the 1984 season and remained a member of the New South Wales organization. However, at the end of the season they were again voted out of the Sydney League, though they have appealed against that decision. Thus, because of financial restraint, the major league in Australia was reduced during 1984 to thirteen teams, though the attempt to expand into areas outside Sydney, with clubs in Canberra and Ilawarra, has proved very successful. Many fans and players actually welcomed the cut-back as being beneficial to the game by producing a shorter season! But no one, surely, can welcome the fall of a club of the stature of Newtown.

It is often the case that when an organization is at its peak it is also at its most vulnerable, and certainly that appeared to be the case with the Australian Rugby League, off the field, in 1983. However, on the field little had changed, for the talents of Mal Meninga and Wally Lewis, the wiles of Peter Sterling and the pace and power of Eric Grothe and Kerry Boustead would still be around for the Test series in Australia in 1984. As the British players trooped off the field at Headingley in the chill of that Sunday in November 1982, in the knowledge that they had lost all three Test matches and had conceded the staggering score of 99 points, few in the team or in the crowd could have thought that within the space of eighteen months Great Britain would be in a position to challenge again with any confidence. The British Rugby League world, badly but rightly shaken, had been stirred into action. But would reforms and new ideas, both on and off the field, be sufficient to bring success in Australia in 1984? The calendar of action was put into operation. As to its effectiveness, only time would tell!

3

THE LIONS PREPARE

December 1982 – May 1983

Though the 1982 Test series in Great Britain attracted large crowds and glowing media coverage and produced outstanding Rugby League skills, albeit from the Australians, it was both an embarrassment and a blessing to the British game. The next six months were well spent by the British Rugby League authorities in introducing a number of new ideas which would help to create the right environment off the field; and they encouraged Dick Gemmell, an ex-Great Britain player and a Hull director, and Frank Myler, the captain of the last Ashes-winning side in 1970, who had been appointed manager and coach respectively of the 1984 touring party, to set about their task on the field with enthusiasm and energy.

Working under the old adage 'A team on the field is only as good as the team off the field', one of the most constructive moves in this period was the consolidation of the National Coaching Scheme under Phil Larder, the ex-Oldham and Whitehaven player. Even though its effect on the preparation of the 1984 tour was not dramatic, it certainly helped. Much good work had been done in the past by various coaching bodies, but a concerted effort was now made during this six-month's period to upgrade the old regional coaching schemes, to assess and learn from other sports bodies and to present a better organized structure in which they could take place. Phil Larder and his regional coaches used the Australian Rugby League coaching courses and the American grid-iron football methods as their guide. Larder even visited Australia and America in 1983 to see their training techniques at first hand. Aided by new coaching manuals, visual aids, specially designed equipment and innovative training methods, more and more emphasis was placed on fitness and individual skills.

Larder and his staff were readily available to the Great Britain squad, and the new coaching methods they were able to pass on played a considerable part in the squad's preparation.

May brought two further innovations, one of which was to have a direct impact on the tour. A new nine-man management committee of the Rugby Football League, while not directly concerned with the forthcoming series, nevertheless dealt with many matters of importance to the management and the squad members. For years the thirty or so representatives from member clubs had been considered too unwieldy a body to run the game efficiently. With its archaic voting structures and with many members regarding the council simply as a talking shop, it had become increasingly difficult to deal quickly with problems of marketing and sponsorship, for example, quite apart from problems within clubs or within the game itself. Consequently, after years of struggle by the secretary-general, the establishment of a much smaller executive to look after the daily running of the sport in terms of international affairs, finance, marketing, sponsorship and so on was a decision of far-reaching importance. Its members – Joe Seddon (St Helens), Brian Pitchford (Warrington), Harry Ditchfield (Widnes), Jack Bateman (Swinton), Reg Parker (Blackpool), Jack Grindrod (Rochdale Hornets), David Wigham (Whitehaven), Bob Ashby (Featherstone Rovers) and Phil Brunt (Castleford) – were to meet every fortnight to deal with such business as had a bearing on the future of the League game. With sponsorship as one of the new committee's areas of concern, its members must have been highly gratified when David Howes, the Rugby League's PRO, was able to announce, also in May, another unprecedented move which was to have a direct bearing on the tour and its preparation.

Remembering that the 1979 tour of Australia and New Zealand, because of a string of poor results, had been a financial disaster, and conscious of the fact that success at Test level generates considerable wealth for the wider good of the game, the authorities were able to announce a generous sponsorship deal for the whole tour. Though the first tour to Australia in 1910 had been helped by Oxo – James Lomas and his team declaring, 'The players agree that for training Oxo is *par excellence*' – this sponsorship agreement was to become the cornerstone of the pre-tour preparations. Modern Maintenance Products, a Harrogate-based company, agreed to underwrite preparations and to aid expenses while the team was abroad to the sum of £35,000, as well as providing £65,000 worth of ground maintenance materials for the benefit of all clubs in the League. With each club allocated almost £2,000 worth of materials, it was with justifiable pride that the chairman of the company, David Brook, asserted that this was 'truly a pioneer sponsorship in aiding the grass roots of the game yet at the same time supporting the vital upper strata – Test rugby'. With the formation of the National Coaching Scheme, the creation of the nine-man management committee and the appointment of a sponsor for the tour, the groundwork had been prepared.

In April 1983 the Rugby League confirmed the appointments of Dick Gemmell and Frank Myler as manager and coach. On the field they were to be responsible for the Under-24 and full international matches against France in the forthcoming season as well as co-ordinating the programme of fitness and training skills prior to the tour. The inclusion of this programme in the tour preparation meant the further appointment of Rod McKenzie, senior lecturer at Carnegie College, Leeds, as fitness consultant, his task being to devise pre-tour and tour fitness programmes for the team.

For the first time in Test history the coach and manager were also given sole responsibility for selecting the squad and were free to take advice from whomever they wished to consult. This surely was a logical step, since over the next twelve months they would be blending their side in trial and international matches and they would also be in a position to determine players' fitness, attitude and character, having spent countless hours in their company. Sadly, in the event the complete freedom of choice given to manager and coach did not provide the touring party with the quality players they needed. The constant changes in the squad, as the months went by – though naturally injuries played an important part – seemed illogical. Certainly there appeared to be no consistent pattern in the selection of players. In any event, before the end of the season, they had named a squad of forty-seven players to train during the summer in the hope that they would be able to select the final tour party from this pool. The squad was drawn from a wide range of clubs:

Bradford Northern:	Ellery Hanley, Keith Mumby, Brian Noble
Castleford:	Kevin Beardmore, Keith England, Gary Hyde, John Joyner, Kevin Ward
Featherstone Rovers:	David Hobbs, Peter Smith, John Gilbert
Hull:	Lee Crooks, Steve Evans, Trevor Skerrett, David Topliss
Hull Kingston Rovers:	Garry Clark, George Fairbairn, Phil Hogan, Mike Smith, David Watkinson
Hunslet:	Graham King
Keighley:	David Moll
Leeds:	Andy Smith
Leigh:	Des Drummond, John Woods
Oldham:	Ray Ashton, Terry Flanagan, Andy Goodway, Mick Worrall
St Helens:	Chris Arkwright, Roy Haggerty, Neil Holding, Gary Moorby

Salford:	Ron Smith
Warrington:	Ron Duane, John Fieldhouse
Widnes:	Mick Adams, Mick Burke, Andy Gregory, David Hulme, Joe Lydon, Tony Myler, Keiron O'Loughlin, Mike O'Neill
Wigan:	Dennis Ramsdale
Workington Town:	Howard Burns, Ian Hartley

When letters naming the squad began to drop through letter boxes in the Ridings of Yorkshire, across the Pennines in Lancashire and in the furthest reaches of Cumbria, to some they came as a surprise and a challenge; to others they were the beginning of a sad experience as players found themselves unable to measure up to the demands expected of them. Such demands were immediately outlined at a squad meeting at Headingley towards the end of May 1983, when Rod McKenzie described his plans prior to the first training weekend. A running schedule of 5 miles, three times per week, plus a weights routine for each individual was to be carried out by the player on his own before all the group appeared at Carnegie College for the first of a series of weekend training camps. The tour diary was now well under way.

June – July 1983

Although the squad had been named, manager Dick Gemmell insisted that any players showing the right attitude and outstanding form during the season, and not included in the first list, would be called up. The converse would also be true. While sympathy was shown to some players for non-attendance, persistent absence at training or continual low fitness levels meant that some players had to be dropped from Frank Myler's plans.

When Rod McKenzie had helped with the teams prior to 1983 the players, invariably the older ones, did not take training as seriously as they might; nor could many of them see the need for such 'new fangled and technical training'. Yet the catastrophic defeats in 1982 against Australia caused a re-think even among the players themselves, especially among the newly emerging crop of youngsters. The veteran stand-off David Topliss (Hull), who was involved in the preparation of both Test series, summed up the attitude for me when I spoke to him at the first training camp. As I held his feet he worked as hard as any youngster to achieve a target of fifty-two sit-ups a minute, yet still had breath left to give me his observations on the different attitudes. 'There is greater enthusiasm than when the Australians beat us in 1982. Here are younger, keener players who want to take part and who are very eager to get fit. Last year many didn't want to know anything about fitness schedules. They merely lazed around and sought the easy way out.' There was certainly no lazing around at the third training camp which I attended at Carnegie College over the weekend of 16 and 17 July!

The two previous camps, beginning on 4 June and 26 June, had given Rod McKenzie a chance to assess the players' levels of fitness. He had been able to prepare work schedules, including a weights routine and stamina and speed running, for each player to undertake at his home club. Such work schedules highlighted the players' weaknesses in relation to the game, as all training at the camps was designed to meet the demands put on the body when playing Rugby League. Thankfully, no demands were put on my body, for the work at the third camp was certainly strenuous and searching in its intensity. When the training camp began at 10.00 a.m. on the Saturday morning there were only thirty-one of the squad present, eight being on holiday, while some like Peter Smith and David Hobbs (both of Featherstone Rovers) were injured. Some players simply did not attend. As Dick Gemmell remarked, 'I don't think they wanted to take the final tests today because they possibly have not maintained the strict training programme which Rod McKenzie outlined for them.' Here at the final camp was the chance to assess the dedication and determination of each member. As with the players of former times, and as with the 1982 Australian tour party, the player's own individual professionalism determined his success or failure.

During the fifteen-minute lecture which started the course, Rod McKenzie soon revealed himself as a disciplinarian, and he commanded respect immediately for his knowledge and no-nonsense approach. Like every good teacher, he explained every facet of, and every reason behind, each exercise and treated his players with respect. He indicated how they were to be made fit for Rugby League and especially for the position in which each played. His explanations, and those of his assistant Tony Gomersall, from York University, who controlled the strength tests, won the confidence of the players. As McKenzie pointed out, it was important that they should 'see the relationship between their exercises and the game of League itself, thereby giving them a greater incentive to train'. With the introductory talk concluded, the real work began.

From 10.15 a.m. to 12.15 p.m. there was no shirking at any of the gymnasium exercises as the players performed an assortment of circuits featuring sit-ups, dips, step-ups and so on. Initially, the mood was quiet, for the players seemed a little wary of each other. The seven Widnes players tended to remain together

4. The determination shown by Great Britain's prop Keith Rayne to break through the Western Division defence at Dubbo, NSW, on 27 May, typifies his commitment in all the matches he played on the tour.

as a group, with the exception of Joe Lydon who was confident of his own abilities and bubbled over with enthusiasm. Soon, however, the competitiveness of the exercises broke down the reserve of many of them, and a player like John Fieldhouse (Warrington) was engaged in friendly rivalry with Kevin Beardmore (Castleford) on the weight exercises. 'How much did you lift?' 'How many dips did you manage?' Such were the questions bandied around the gymnasium. And with each player having to carry out an exercise under the eyes of the others in his group, he was forced to perform to his utmost. Within the groups individual players were made to take on responsibility by coaching the others and by seeing that each was doing the exercises correctly. As Rod McKenzie had planned, 'The group expanded from training an individual to providing corporate responsibility for the good of the party as a whole.' Here was the same type of thinking that lay behind the 1982 Australian party's training programme. Whether such thoughts were going through the mind of Widnes scrum-half Andy Gregory, valiantly struggling on a last exercise of dips and being sarcastically encouraged by Brian Noble, the Bradford hooker, was debatable. 'It's only pain, Andy, it's nowt!'

When the time came to leave the gymnasium to run 1,500 metres on a specially marked grass track, the club groupings and loyalties had been replaced by squad loyalty. During this 1,500-metre run test the players actively encouraged and jeered at each other from the sidelines. A corporate spirit built up among the squad when the onlookers urged on Ellery Hanley to a time of 4 minutes and 20 seconds, or when Ray Ashton raced alongside his club mate, Terry Flanagan, with words of encouragement. There was also considerable humour at the sight of the short, chunky Andy Gregory and the tall Ian Hartley struggling in last on the stamina run. For two hours and three-quarters they did not relax until a welcome cup of hot, sweet tea at 1.00 p.m. brought respite. But within half an hour Tony Gomersall had the players arranged on an incredible array of weight and strength machines, all specially adapted for the situations players would encounter in a game. One such machine had an assortment of weights to be raised by the shoulders. This exercise, usually performed by a player while lying on his back on a sloping bench, now had to be undertaken by the player lying on his stomach in order to develop strength for scrummaging and tackling. Keith England, the young Castleford colt, certainly helped to develop his shoulder and leg muscles as he grappled with a weight of 550 pounds in this forward position.

Following the stamina and strength tests, and after a short warm-up, the players once again vied with each other over a series of 30- and 40-metre sprints and shuttle runs. Though the speedy Leigh winger and BBC-TV Superstars' 100-metre champion, Des Drummond, was expected to be the fastest over the electronically timed 40-metre circuit, it was Joe Lydon, confident as ever, who took the honours with a time of 4.69 seconds. Stung into action, Des Drummond sprinted home the winner over 30 metres with 3.78 seconds. When I visited the training camp, it was clear that the players were working very hard. Most had enjoyed the physical demands placed upon them, and as Gary Moorby remarked, 'It's not boring. It's very enjoyable.' Each player, I am sure, could sense the purpose behind the day's activities and could appreciate the results.

During my short visit, and especially over the six-week initial training period, the squad had developed as a unit, proud of its progress. Spirits were high and were helped by the humour of the players themselves, as when Ron Duane tried to breathe in during the 'fat' tests, sadly for him with no effect on the excess held in the calipers on his stomach. It remained to be seen whether the players could accept the responsibility for their fitness which the management now placed upon them by issuing each with a training schedule to be continued at his home club during the coming season. If they did not, there would be little hope for them. As Rod McKenzie made clear, 'Prior to the selection of the international teams to play against France the squad will be retested to check that players are not slipping back in their fitness training.'

During all this activity the manager, Dick Gemmell, moved around asking players their reasons whenever they had pulled up short on an exercise, inquiring about ailments and adding the odd friendly comment, especially when late in the day he mildly chided Rod McKenzie who seemed never to stop. 'What will they have for dinner, Rod?' he asked. 'They've trained hard and only had one cup of tea since 10.00 a.m.'

Some players trained harder than others over this initial six-week period, but none escaped the eye of McKenzie who recorded every detail of the players' progress. Whether they had been diligent, as in the case of Ray Ashton, for example, whose report is reproduced here, or whether they had been one of those whose personal profile charts urged greater application as the season opened, all received their 'end-of-term report'.

RAY ASHTON – SCRUM-HALF

Name of test	date	initial score	initial grade	date	retest score	retest grade	date	retest score	retest grade
Running stamina 12-min. run	4/6/83	3085m	good	26/6/83	3113m	good			
Sprint speed 40 metres	4/6/83	5.43 secs	average					5.17	good
Flexibility sit and reach test	4/6/83	9.6	average				16/7/83	12.5	good
Muscular endurance Leg lifts (30 secs)	4/6/83	30	good	26/6/83	29	good	16/7/83	35	very good
Muscular endurance Pull ups (1 min. max)	4/6/83	12	average	26/6/83	20	very good	16/7/83	21	very good
Muscular endurance Sit ups (1 min.)	4/6/83	48	average	26/6/83	59	good	16/7/83	63	very good
Muscular endurance Dips (1 min. max)	4/6/83	16	average	26/6/83	33	good	16/7/83	35	good
Percentage fat	4/6/83	14.05	average	26/6/83	12.4		16/7/83	12.4	

Excellent progress has been made over the summer. It is vital this is maintained during the season. R. McKenzie

I am sure that Rod McKenzie won the confidence of the players in those early days. It was a sign of his success that he was able to praise the squad's efforts in a personal letter to every member, even though he had to express doubts in one area of fitness which would have to be rectified during the season:

> 'The tests suggested that running stamina is one of the weakest aspects of the squad's fitness, and even though the emphasis in training at this stage of the season should be on sprinting, it is important to undertake one endurance run per week. After all it is running stamina which allows a player to perform as well at the end of the game as at the beginning.'

September 1983

Although the fitness of the intended tour party was to be one of the priorities in all this preparatory work, Frank Myler himself said, 'It must not be the sole requirement for selection.' The management's task was first to select a squad of players for their rugby ability and then to ensure that they had the necessary fitness to enhance their skills. It was with this in mind that the management agreed to play two trial games in the early part of the season with a view to assessing the strengths or weaknesses of the original squad selection. Though not a new idea – trials had been held in the 1950s before every overseas tour – it was a welcome one. A trial can put players on their mettle; and players from weaker clubs can compete on the same footing as those from the strongest. Many would have preferred public trials, but the decision to play the games in private was taken at the request of the coach who wished to rearrange and substitute his players while the game was in progress (though one might question the wisdom of that). However, with the cancellation of the first trial through injuries, fixture congestion and holidays, and with the disruption of the second, again by injuries, it was decided to hold the second trial behind closed doors – perhaps with disastrous consequences for subsequent team selection.

The trial, held at Swinton on 6 September, hardly filled me with confidence. When I arrived at 5.30 p.m., an hour before kick-off, I was greeted by a large group of players standing behind the main stand and discussing injuries incurred in the previous matches. Many, like Mike O'Neill (Widnes), had obvious injuries and were visibly upset at being unable to play, but others seemed relieved at being unfit to take part. Frank Myler looked harassed and concerned at the number of players who had arrived claiming an injury; and it was only after a late telephone call to the Warrington second-row forward Bob

40

5. Joe Lydon, Andy Gregory, Ellery Hanley, Des Drummond and Garry Schofield always trained enthusiastically – here under the tall buildings surrounding Sydney's Domain – despite the gruelling schedules they were put through. Credit must go to Rod McKenzie for the carefully planned and imaginatively thought out sessions which maintained the interest of the players throughout the Australian section of the tour.

Eccles that he was able to assemble a full complement of twenty-six players to start the game. The start had to be delayed as some of the players had difficulty in fitting on borrowed boots. Eventually the Reds kicked off, faced by ten men of the Greens, surrounded by eerie, deserted terraces around which every voice from the pitch could be heard. After urgent exhortations from Frank Myler, the Greens quickly assembled their full complement of players, some in unaccustomed positions.

In the early stages of the game the Greens dominated the proceedings through good scrum possession from Noble and shrewd distribution from Holding. Indeed, it was Holding, playing at stand-off, who created two of the three tries scored in the opening twenty minutes by Hyde and Smith, while his partner at scrum-half, Ray Ashton, made a second for Smith after a neat short kick had hoodwinked the Reds' defence. A conversion from Mumby gave the match a very one-sided look at 14–0. The Reds, with their loose-forward, Terry Flanagan, especially prominent, were concentrating too much on intricate forward play down the middle. Here the second-row forwards, Hobbs and Haggarty, could make little ground against the solid defence of Goodway and Skerrett in particular. Little seemed to have been learned from Great Britain's experiences against the Australian defences until in the final ten minutes of the half the Reds moved the ball out wider, where Joyner was able to send Topliss over for a try, which Lydon converted. Sensing at last that there were gaps on the flanks, the Reds attacked again down the same flank, where Clark rounded off a fine move on the wing, gaining the better of both Ledger and Mumby on his way to the try-line. The half-time score of 14–10 in the Greens' favour reflected an evenly balanced game, but few had staked any real claim to an Australian trip, save perhaps Hanley and Mumby, both of whom looked very strong when on the break.

With the effervescent Widnes scrum-half, Andy Gregory, having come on the field at loose-forward for the Reds in place of the injured Eccles, the pack had a strange look about it in the second half. This was even more pronounced when, after numerous players had transferred between sides, David Watkinson, the hooker, was forced to leave the field with no other player available to replace him. It was therefore no surprise that despite a cheeky try and conversion from Gregory, the Reds, with only twelve men, were forced to concede further tries from Ledger and Holding. A conversion by Holding to his own try brought the final score to 24–16 for the Greens and underlined their superiority. But I am sure the coach could not have been happy at the performance of some of the players. Afterwards, at the hot-pot prepared for all the squad in the clubhouse, it was significant that the coach and the manager were locked in deep discussion with Phil Larder, the national coaching director, who had assembled a mass of statistics about the game. Frank Myler had learned much about the attitude of some of the players, both on and off the field. He had witnessed some of the squad fail to come up to the standards expected, but at least he was a wiser man after the trial than before.

Greens: Mumby (Bradford Northern); Hyde (Castleford), Hanley (Bradford Northern), Smith (Hull KR), Ledger (St Helens); Holding (St Helens), Ashton (Oldham); Skerrett (Hull), Noble (Bradford Northern), Goodway (Oldham), Moorby (Leeds), Hartley (Workington Town), Crane (Hull)

Reds: Lydon (Widnes); Clark (Hull KR), Joyner (Castleford), O'Loughlin (Widnes), Ramsdale (Wigan); Topliss (Hull), Burns (Workington Town); Eccles (Warrington), Watkinson (Hull KR), England (Castleford), Hobbs (Featherstone Rovers), Haggarty (St Helens), Flanagan (Oldham)

October 1983 – December 1983

By October Frank Myler had begun to understand many of the problems which had not been apparent to him when he took on the job of Great Britain's coach. Myler had accepted the position because, as he said, 'I was disgusted with the players' attitude in the 1979 and 1982 series against Australia.' He had approached the task without arrogance, in fact the reverse, for he intended 'to set the ball rolling by going for younger players who are proud and dedicated and who, if beaten, will come back as the nucleus to create our future attitudes'. Frank Myler's aims were laudable, especially his attitude to the type of player to be selected. Like Albert Pimblett in 1948 and Wayne Pearce in 1982, he too firmly believed that despite training camps and organized sessions, 'The player has to discipline himself. If a player has the correct attitude, he will get himself fit.'

Though most clubs in this early stage of the season were helpful, Myler was disappointed at the inability of the players to meet as a squad more often. He was further disappointed at the squad sessions and trial game, where the attitude of some of the players failed to come up to his expectations. These he noted as unsuitable tourists, though to his credit he always retained an open mind, and his eventual tour selection to some extent reflected his earlier promise to pick men in form as the season developed. His training squads were to be no 'closed shop' for the original tour party. Many were critical of his decision not to play a match against Queensland, who made a short tour of northern England in October, but I think he was right not to tackle this fine side. As Myler said, 'We are still in the formative stage. My work is still in progress. Why shatter my players' confidence when we are still putting time in on the training field and fitness circuits?'

The management of the 1984 tour party had stressed the great importance of the Under-24 matches against France at Villeneuve on Friday, 11 November 1983, and the return at Oldham on Sunday, 4 December. Hence the weekly sessions held for the younger players would prove the making or undoing of many. Such sessions, like the one I saw at Oldham, were designed more for tactical appreciation and for the moulding of the nucleus of a tour squad than for fitness, as were the meetings at Carnegie College. Fitness was now being left principally to the individual himself, though this was monitored regularly by Rod McKenzie at the Oldham sessions.

On the Wednesday prior to the match at Villeneuve, Phil Larder and Frank

Myler spent only an hour, from 7.15 to 8.15 p.m., on the pitch, having for the previous half-hour been at the fitness checks in the multi-purpose gymnasium at the Oldham clubhouse. Myler's thinking up to the point when he actually named the squad was dominated by the need for sound defence. Exhaustive sessions were spent, usually of two minutes' continuous duration, in which the players hammered at the tackling shields held by their colleagues. Though requiring much physical exertion, perhaps the word 'hammered' is the wrong one to use, for, unlike the Kangaroos in 1982, I felt that many of the players were merely going through the motions. The solid thud, to be heard all round the Australians' training area, was missing at Oldham. I think Phil Larder felt this too, as he urged greater commitment. Frank Myler also tried to whip up aggression as he took part in semi-opposed rugby, once again laying great stress on the defensive patterns needed and the urgency of the team moving up quickly in line together.

Following a short fifteen-minute physical session from Rod McKenzie, the players were leaving the field by 8.15 p.m. Many barriers were obviously breaking down between the Under-24 players during these weekly meetings, and team spirit was building up, but I sensed that a minority of the players still did not appreciate the demands expected of them by the management. They soon did, following France's record score against them, even though Great Britain enjoyed their twelfth consecutive Under-24 victory, 28–23.

Admittedly, Britain, whether through injury or suspension, were deprived of players who were to become tourists, like Tony Myler, Andy Gregory, Andy Goodway, Lee Crooks and Ellery Hanley, but the defence, described by one press critic as 'geriatric', left a lot to be desired. On the attacking front only Ray Ashton's hat-trick of tries revealed any real promise. But the message had got through, and in the return match a much stronger side, more akin to Myler's original selection, showed steel in its defence and flair in its attack in annihilating France 48–1 at Oldham. With Joe Lydon beating the points record for an Under-24 match with 20, and with Tony Myler collecting a hat-trick of tries, the team displayed enough quality rugby for Louis Bonnery, the French coach, to declare, 'It was the most professional display I have seen from a British team for many years.' This game revealed all that Frank Myler had been seeking – youthful exuberance allied to skill in attack and defence. Myler had declared before the game, 'Anybody who doesn't do the job properly can forget about the tour', but after the match, though he made no comment, I am convinced he had already pencilled in twelve of the fifteen players who had appeared that day – only Barry Ledger (St Helens), Brian Dunn (Wigan) and John Fieldhouse (Warrington) did not make the eventual selection. With Trevor Skerrett (Hull) named as the tour captain and with Rod McKenzie appointed 'fitness consultant' for the duration of the tour, by the end of

December there was light at the end of what had seemed a very dark tunnel. The next series of matches against the full French side in January and February 1984 was felt by many to darken the prospect somewhat, but even here I felt that the management learned much, albeit in a negative sense.

January – February 1984

The selection of prop forward Trevor Skerrett as tour captain well in advance of the naming of the tour party had been indicated to me privately by Frank Myler as early as October 1983. In assessing the requirements for a successful tour captain, Myler said that he needed a player who had been to Australia before and who knew exactly the demands of Test rugby. Following the disastrous tour of Australia in 1979, it was obvious that there were few candidates, and of these Trevor Skerrett was the natural choice, being one of the few players who was certain of a Test place.

Sadly for Skerrett, his hopes of captaining the tour were dashed by knee cartilage trouble, while many fancied contenders failed to live up to expectations after the two Great Britain victories over France, 12–0 at Avignon on 29 January and 10–0 at Headingley on 17 February. The defence at Avignon had once again been first-class, and Keith Rayne (Leeds) sprang to prominence as a prop-forward candidate by taking the man-of-the-match award. But sadly, David Watkinson, the Hull KR hooker, ruined his tour chances by fracturing his leg. Plans for the tour, which had been progressing reasonably smoothly, now seemed to run into trouble, and February and the remaining months of preparation were to provide Myler and Gemmell with more headaches than had the previous fifteen months. But again I firmly believe that they learned from all that happened.

When the Rugby Football League announced a forty-one-man 'training squad' on 1 February, surprisingly different from the original selection and again drawing charges of inconsistency on to manager and coach, they countered this criticism, explaining that the list was by no means the final party. Indeed, little did they realize how few of those named would actually make the tour. Many would train at Huddersfield over the next ten weeks, but sixteen of the squad would fall by the wayside. These were the names included in the 'training squad':

Full-backs:	Mick Burke (Widnes), George Fairbairn (Hull KR), Keith Mumby (Bradford Northern)
Three-quarters:	John Basnett (Widnes), Garry Clark (Hull KR), Des Drummond (Leigh), Ron Duane (Warrington), Steve Evans (Hull), Des Foy (Oldham), John Joyner (Castleford), Joe Lydon (Widnes), Garry Schofield (Hull), Mike Smith (Hull KR)
Half-backs:	John Woods (Leigh), Ellery Hanley (Bradford Northern), Tony Myler (Widnes), Ray Ashton (Oldham), David Cairns (Barrow), Andy Gregory (Widnes)
Forwards:	Andy Goodway (Oldham), Mike and Steve O'Neill (Widnes), Keith Rayne (Leeds), Trevor Skerrett (Hull), Chris Burton (Hull KR), Len Casey (Hull KR), Lee Crooks (Hull), Brian Noble (Bradford Northern), Andy Dannatt (Hull), David Hobbs (Featherstone Rovers), Dick Jasiewicz (Bradford Northern), Peter Smith (Featherstone Rovers), Kevin Ward (Castleford), Fred Whitfield (Widnes), John Wood (Widnes), Mick Worrall (Oldham), Mick Adams (Widnes), Terry Flanagan (Oldham), David Hall (Hull KR), Alan Rathbone (Bradford Northern)

With the Challenge Cup in its final stages, Frank Myler was once again confronted with problems of club versus country loyalty. Faced with the refusal by Widnes to release nine of their ten players for training before the full international match with France at Headingley, Myler seemed determined to pursue a policy of 'no training, no play' and promptly axed them from his selection. Only John Basnett, who did train, was selected. Arguments were such within the Widnes club and at Bradford, where coach Peter Fox followed suit with a refusal to release his players, that Harry Dawson, the popular Widnes coach, resigned from the club following a disagreement with the manager, Vince Karalius, over his refusal. Myler's decision was right in principle, though one felt sorry for the helpless players whose coach or manager had prevented them from being able to put country before club. What Karalius and Fox should have accepted was that the national side must come first. Rugby must be seen as a pyramid with the clubs as the solid base, not as a pyramid turned upside-down with the clubs on top. I could sympathize, too, with Myler and Gemmell, for though they removed nine Widnes men from the Headingley match, most realists knew that they could not remove such talented players from the tour. Eventually, time healed the rift, though ironically John Basnett, the only one to turn up for training, was left out of the final tour selection.

6.   Use of the tackle shield is now an essential element in training. The Lions are shown here driving into their shields, during a session on Sydney's Domain, though perhaps with rather less relish than the Australians always brought to this aspect of their training.

Basnett was not the only player to fall from grace after Britain's below-par defeat of France on that Friday evening at Headingley. Though the critics savaged Myler's preparation when Britain flopped badly, the with-drawal of the Widnes players again allowed experiments to be made in the side with the result that many, especially in the forwards, were found wanting at the highest level. Surely it is better to discover in February who is not good enough than to learn too late in Australia. Sadly for Frank Myler, as the next three months proved, he was to learn who would be on tour only twenty-four hours before their departure from Heathrow Airport on Sunday, 13 May.

March – May 1984

Though Myler's plans for deciding his final tour party must have been affected by the unavailability of David Hall (Hull KR), John Woods (Leigh) and Steve Evans (Hull), all of whom withdrew from the squad, he was obviously not too much concerned. 'At least I will have players around me who are keen to go and will have no worries about leaving the country for three months,' was his assessment of the withdrawals. With other players pulling out, Brian Case (Wigan) and Harry Pinner (St Helens), whose late season form had prompted many, including myself, to question their original absence, were now brought into the squad. Here were two forwards who were eager and proud to represent Great Britain. It was the enforced withdrawals on the eve of departure that really troubled the management – withdrawals which were to stir controversy and leave ripples of discontent long after the party had taken to the air.

The announcement that the original tour skipper Trevor Skerrett had failed in his struggle to recover from ligament trouble heaped up problems on top of the unavailability of Peter Smith (Featherstone Rovers), also unable to recover in time from back trouble. Skerrett's withdrawal was the bigger headache for suddenly, with only a couple of weeks to departure, the tour was without a captain. Frank Myler had insisted upon an experienced man to captain his tourists and had urged an early appointment, but now he was forced to turn to Brian Noble, the Bradford Northern hooker. Noble, at 23 years of age and with only four Great Britain caps behind him, was to be the youngest ever Lions tour captain – so much for experience! In truth, with only four members surviving from the ill-fated 1979 tour, there were few players to take on the role. I do not deride the choice of Noble as captain because, if experience was now no longer available to him, then Myler was right to opt for youthful energy and leadership by example. Throughout the preparation for the tour none had shown himself better fitted for such a role than Noble, and only time would tell how he would respond on tour with a young party around him with an average age of 24. Then came the news that the Rugby Football League had withdrawn Len Casey (Hull KR) from the party.

A six-month ban imposed on Casey for pushing a touch judge in a televised league game aroused controversy. And the ill-feeling was followed by even greater discontent in the next few days. Despite Casey's attempt, by taking his appeal to the High Court, to restrain the League from imposing the six-month suspension, Mr Justice Drake in Leeds ruled that the disciplinary rules were lawful and that the ban was not excessive. Casey was therefore ruled out of the tour, and with only a week to go Chris Arkwright (St Helens) and Wayne

Proctor (Hull) were drafted into yet another revised squad. Yet just five days before the party was due to leave, Chris Arkwright, the 25-year-old utility player, was withdrawn following a fitness test. Although the St Helens club doctors had passed him fit, when Arkwright was asked to undergo stringent fitness tests along with the other tourists, the League's own specialist revealed damage to a knee. This cruel blow stirred considerable ill-feeling in Arkwright's home town, especially when Tony Myler, who had undergone a cartilage operation five weeks before departure and had not played a game in the period, was declared fit.

The reasoning behind those two seemingly paradoxical decisions was that Myler's injury had been operated upon and he was responding well. It was thought that he would be fully fit for the early part of the tour, while Arkwright's condition would be aggravated by the trip. It was a strange decision in view of statements made back in 1983 that no player would be taken who was not fully fit on the day of departure. The selection was obviously a huge gamble on the management's part, and one which would no doubt surface again should any problems occur. Of course, everyone realized Tony Myler's value to the tour party – but if Chris Arkwright had had a history of knee trouble throughout the season, why had he not been given a fitness test prior to inclusion? This surely would have avoided the more unpleasant aspects of the affair and saved Arkwright from a late disappointment.

In any event, this was the party that was eventually announced:

Manager: Dick Gemmell   Fitness director: Rod McKenzie
Business manager: Roland Davis   Physiotherapist: Ron Barritt
Coach: Frank Myler

Backs: Ray Ashton (Oldham), Mick Burke (Widnes), Garry Clark (Hull KR), Steve Donlan (Leigh), Des Drummond (Leigh), Ron Duane (Warrington), Des Foy (Oldham), Andy Gregory (Widnes), Ellery Hanley (Bradford Northern), Neil Holding (St Helens), John Joyner (Castleford), Joe Lydon (Widnes), Keith Mumby (Bradford Northern), Tony Myler (Widnes), Garry Schofield (Hull), Mike Smith (Hull KR)

Forwards: Mick Adams (Widnes), Kevin Beardmore (Castleford), Chris Burton (Hull KR), Brian Case (Wigan), Lee Crooks (Hull), Terry Flanagan (Oldham), Andy Goodway (Oldham), David Hobbs (Featherstone Rovers), Brian Noble (Bradford Northern), captain, Mike O'Neill (Widnes), Harry Pinner (St Helens), Wayne Proctor (Hull), Keith Rayne (Leeds), Mick Worrall (Oldham)

(A late addition to the party was to be John Basnett (Widnes), who flew out to take the place of Ron Duane, forced to return home after being injured in the very first match of the tour.)

As with all tour selections, the discussions aroused by the choice were endless, but at least the days of waiting were over. The total commitment to, and pride in, the Great Britain jersey which Frank Myler had urged on the players throughout the long period of preparation were clearly shown by Neil Holding's reaction to selection: 'I couldn't sleep the night before. Then the letter came on that Monday morning in a brown envelope from Rugby League headquarters. I stood at the bottom of the stairs in the hall, staring at it on the floor, frightened to open it. When I did, I couldn't take the good news in until about three o'clock that afternoon.'

Whether there were sufficient players within the squad of thirty with the necessary skills only time would tell, though with teenagers such as Joe Lydon, Garry Clark and Garry Schofield, the party was certainly as fit as, if not fitter than, any touring party sent abroad before.

Though in the event a number of the players selected were shown not to have been good enough, at least Frank Myler thought he had chosen the best available to play to the requirements of the new sixth-tackle turnover rule, which had become operative the previous September. Any Test side must be designed to take maximum advantage of the laws, and the handing of the ball to the opposition after the sixth tackle has created a faster and more varied game. With defence as a priority men like Goodway, O'Neill, Crooks and Worrall were looked on as the tacklers, while it was hoped that loose forwards Adams and Pinner would relish the increased opportunities for broken play and tactical kicking. Under the new law the 1983–84 season in Britain had revealed the need for greater pace, and here, though the speed of Drummond and Lydon, among the backs, equalled that of any of the Australians, there was a distinct lack of pace among the forwards. Britain seemed to lack true second-row runners with the ball, but I doubt whether I could have found others elsewhere in the League to match the size and pace of the Australians and the New Zealanders. It was significant that Frank Myler was obviously aware of this problem and had, as he said, based his selections on an acceptance of the weakness, 'We have enough pace if the forwards work as a unit. We have the men who can stop the opposition.'

With regard to the players' basic skills, it was felt by most observers that among the backs, players like Burke, Gregory and Hanley possessed true footballing ability, and that the rapidly maturing talent of youngsters like Schofield, Lydon, Clark and Duane would blossom on tour. A sensible feature, too, in the selection of the backs was the inclusion of proven utility players like Donlan, Smith and Joyner, all of whom could play in a number of positions.

The importance of the tour to the future of Rugby League in Great Britain, shattered during the series with Australia two years before, was reflected in the attitude of manager Dick Gemmell: 'This tour is not going to be a picnic. We are not taking passengers. We must win.' Would they?

4

THE LIONS IN AUSTRALIA:
TO THE FIRST TEST

The impact of the tackle made by Keith Rayne on the North Sydney prop Don McKinnon in the fiftieth minute of the fifth match of the Lions' tour at the Sydney Cricket Ground caused a shudder to reverberate round the sparsely filled grandstands. The force of the tackle, delivered straight to the midriff, even caused a lone Union Jack to be raised aloft on the notorious 'hill'. The ball spun loose from McKinnon's grasp to be retrieved by an eager Kevin Beardmore, the Great Britain hooker. A sigh of relief was to be heard from the British press contingent, caused not by the fact that the Lions had withstood ten minutes of the most ferocious forward running from North Sydney, but by the knowledge that at last a British side seemed capable of defending.

Britain had led 14–0 at half-time through two tries with three goals from Mick Burke. The first try in the tenth minute was a well-worked movement over 50 yards by Gregory and Schofield before winger Des Drummond finished it off with a typical burst of speed. The second came from the second-row forward, Andy Goodway, who burst through three tackles to score from 30 yards out. Despite conceding two late tries on the wings, the importance of this fifth victory in Australia far exceeded a win over North Sydney. After the defensive disasters experienced by the British teams in the last two series against Australia, in 1979 and 1982, the tackling of forwards Beardmore, Crooks and Adams was to give a huge psychological boost to the squad and to make the cynical Australian press realize at last that the 1984 Lions meant business. The words of the former Australian loose forward, Johnny Raper, echoed popular opinion on the night when he declared: 'They are no longer soft in the belly and will stretch Australia.'

Whether the Lions would or would not 'stretch Australia' remained to be seen, but this first win at the Sydney Cricket Ground since the second Test of

7. 'Welcome to Sydney!' Mick Adams, the Great Britain loose forward, is given an uncompromising greeting by North Sydney's forwards during the tourists' first match in Sydney on 30 May.

1974 was indicative of the progress that had been made after the rather shaky but still unbeaten start to the tour. In the victories over Northern Territory 40–13, Riverina 22–18, North Coast 56–6 and Western Division 36–30, coach Frank Myler had taken the opportunity to give all the members of his squad an early match. He also used these country games to try out various possible combinations for the first Test. Contrary to pre-tour predictions there appeared to be fewer problems in the forwards than had been expected, and with players like Crooks and Goodway producing forty and fifty tackles a match, the prospects looked bright. Burton and the two hookers, Noble, the captain, and his understudy Beardmore, had revealed an appetite for hard work, while the loose forwards, Pinner and Adams, had both shown flashes of their ball-playing skills. In contrast, the pre-tour optimism which had surrounded the backs suffered a little, as these early matches revealed at times a lack of physical commitment.

The loss of the Warrington centre, Ron Duane, with damaged knee ligaments, in the ninth minute of the first game against Northern Territory, was a blow, but it was an even bigger shock when he was forced to return home after the first Test without taking any further part in the tour. The problems surrounding the Widnes stand-off, Tony Myler, emphasized the lack of real physical strength in midfield, a necessity when facing modern Australian midfield players. Duane's departure meant a summons for the Widnes wing, John Basnett, whom many considered unlucky not to have been included in the original selection. Myler had recovered sufficiently from his cartilage operation for him to be able to play for part of the match against Western Division at Dubbo, but in the following week he suffered inflammation round the suspect knee and had further problems with a calf muscle. Despite a course of tablets and intensive treatment under the physiotherapist, Ron Barritt, together with much swimming and massage treatment at Tattersalls club in Sydney, he too was ruled out of selection for the first Test.

Switching the full-back Keith Mumby to centre for the North Sydney game, where he partnered the young but strong defensive centre Garry Schofield, was to prove a decisive factor in Britain's defensive strategy. Mumby had the physical presence to match the strong running Australian centres, and it was here, as much as in the pack, that the foundations were laid for the fifth win which offered such hopeful signs for the rest of the tour. Whatever the chances of success, the Lions' dedication and ambition in the opening weeks had to be admired. With five wins from five matches there was at last the promise of an outstanding Test series.

For manager and coach the North Sydney game was the first real test of all that they had been working towards during the past eighteen months. Encouraged, too, by a sympathetic Australian press, and heartened by the words of John Hayes, the North Sydney coach – 'To be truthful they did surprise me for their forward defence was strong. They were very committed' – the whole squad eagerly approached their training programme for the final game before the first Test. Indeed, despite groans of despair from Mick Burke whenever Rod McKenzie moved the players from the Sydney hotel foyer to their training ground across the road, all the party, and none more so than Mick himself, tackled the physical sessions with enthusiasm.

Conscious of the Lions' physical limitations in the previous two series, Rod McKenzie had shown himself a harsh task master immediately the party had arrived at Darwin, demanding training sessions three times a day. A pre-breakfast jog of 5 miles greeted all the players at 7 a.m., and woe betide anyone who overslept. The run was designed more as a discipline for the training programme than as a physical fitness aid but, whatever its purpose, it put the players in the right frame of mind for the two arduous sessions later in the morning and in the afternoon. The programme in Darwin had been designed to accustom the players to working in the intense heat and humidity, but uppermost in the minds of Rod McKenzie and Frank Myler, who supervised every session, was the necessity to work on the team's defence and the players' individual speeds. For defence, it is obvious that intensive work on the tackle pads is not sufficient by itself. To perform a succession of tackles, a player must have stamina as well. Therefore, besides group sessions of pounding into the tackle pads, the players also had to run the distances their playing positions meant they were likely to cover in a match. Speed and stamina were developed. A typical set of exercises for the group of centres was particularly gruelling in the heat of a Sydney winter – usually 70°F. Running downhill in an effort to gain a sense of speed, Lydon, Smith, Joyner and company performed nine runs of 30 yards, six runs of 40 yards, four runs of 50 yards and two runs of 60 yards, then they reversed the order of the set distances and repeated the runs over again. Alongside that group, a quartet of prop forwards – Rayne, O'Neill, Case and Crooks – were suffering a similar fate, their distances again geared to distances expected of them in a match. They had to undertake six runs of 10 yards, five runs of 20 yards, four runs of 30 yards, two runs of 40 yards, and then complete the stint by running all the distances again in the reverse order.

It is no wonder that one of the regular features of a morning or afternoon session was the sight of Ron Barritt either spraying the players' faces with water from his 'fly spray' canister or dispensing cups of a thirst-quenching liquid from a barrel at the side of the training area. This liquid, used by American athletes to put salts back into the body, gave welcome relief, especially after another exercise designed to aid sprinting – the 'harness'. The sight of Neil Holding striving to race downfield while held in a harness from behind by little Andy Gregory reminded me of a trotting horse and its jockey or two youngsters struggling to get out of a 'baby bouncer'. Whatever the appearance, the exercise certainly developed thigh muscles and improved the players' speed.

So hard were the physical sessions that the tactical sessions with the ball, under Frank Myler, were greeted with enthusiasm by the exhausted players. These ball practices were often linked to the requirements of a particular game or to strengthen the deficiencies highlighted by a previous match. On the Thursday following the North Sydney game, for example, Myler had groups of five, each led by a player to give him increased responsibility, running with and then dropping the ball. Players nearest to the dropped ball were encouraged to dive on and smother it with their bodies, which Britain had failed to do against North Sydney.

Whatever the emphasis on the physical fitness of a player, Rod McKenzie was conscious of the need to marry the physical with the mental and it was interesting to see introduced for the first time an American idea in sports psychology. At training, the players were encouraged to memorize and use slogans like 'tackling tames Wallies' and 'when the going gets tough, the tough

8. Des Foy listens intently to coach Frank Myler during training at the Domain, Sydney, in preparation for the first Test against Australia. Foy made his international debut in this match.

get going'. The word 'Wally', a derogatory term in Britain, was used rather than 'Aussie', as the latter was thought to belong, by historical association, to super-fit and powerful teams.

The words of the Newcastle coach, Terry Panowitz, delivered after the match against his team, were testimony to the success of the training programme during the six-match pre-Test run: 'Without any doubt they are the fittest British touring team I have seen play.' The trip to Newcastle, via the coastal highway, and the game itself were further indications that the other vital factors, team spirit and morale, were in good shape, fostered by skipper Brian Noble. Though Rod McKenzie's motivational music tape, featuring 'Rule Britannia' and 'Land of Hope and Glory', received an encouraging response, it was Andy Goodway's pop music cassettes which humoured the players. The best vocal rendering was reserved for Frank Sinatra's 'Ant Song' from the film

A Hole in the Head. As with the ant, who in the song has 'high hopes', so the Great Britain party had high hopes of a clean sweep of matches prior to the first Test and were in high spirits after the 100-mile coach journey from Sydney to the International Sports Centre at Newcastle.

With a squad of thirty players many are not involved in the actual match. The problem then arises of what they are to do so that they do not feel redundant. The 1982 Australians solved this problem by making sure everyone had a particular job to do on match days. It was good to see that Britain now followed suit. Not just at Newcastle, but throughout the tour, Brian Noble's organization of baggage men, laundry men, match statistics checkers and gate checkers was a credit to his quiet but effective control, and this helped to create a strong feeling of party unity. Perhaps his orders were obeyed too implicitly by some of his players, as in the case of Mick Burke when acting as a gate checker at Darwin. Noble and the business manager, Roland Davis – a 'hard Pommie' in the words of one Australian club secretary – had organized a team of four players to check the takings at the turnstiles at each match. As the players were to receive a bonus if the tour ended in profit, Noble knew they would be conscientious in their task, but he was a little surprised by Mick Burke's strictness. One poor mother had to pay a $4 entrance fee to recover her little son, who had been playing in a pre-match 'curtain raiser', from the changing rooms!

The spectators at the Newcastle match on 2 June, though obviously upset by a dull performance from the home team, certainly saw some tries from the Lions which were worth $4 entrance money from anyone. With Britain experiencing problems with their handling and team work in the opening twenty minutes, the Newcastle full-back, Neville Elwin, was able to take advantage of some careless play. The Lions' frustrations, and over-eagerness to use the whistle by the referee, Barry Priest, presented Elwin with three simple shots at goal from offside offences and infringements at play-the-balls. At 6–0 in Newcastle's favour, the situation looked ominous for Britain until two tries in the space of three minutes in the twentieth and twenty-third minutes, both showing the value of speed, put Britain ahead 12–6 for the first time in the match. It was the experimental pairing at half-back of Garry Schofield and Neil Holding which did the trick. Schofield sliced through the Newcastle cover from 30 yards out, passed to the loose forward, Flanagan, who cleverly drew the full-back before returning the pass inside for Schofield to collect and score wide out to the left of the posts. Holding's darting 30-yard run three minutes later, when he shot through a gap in the centre, again illustrated the vital difference between the two sides – speed. With Flanagan again backing up well, it was the easiest of tasks for Holding to draw the cover and put him in for a well deserved try. Mick Burke converted both.

Coach Frank Myler was also trying yet another centre combination in

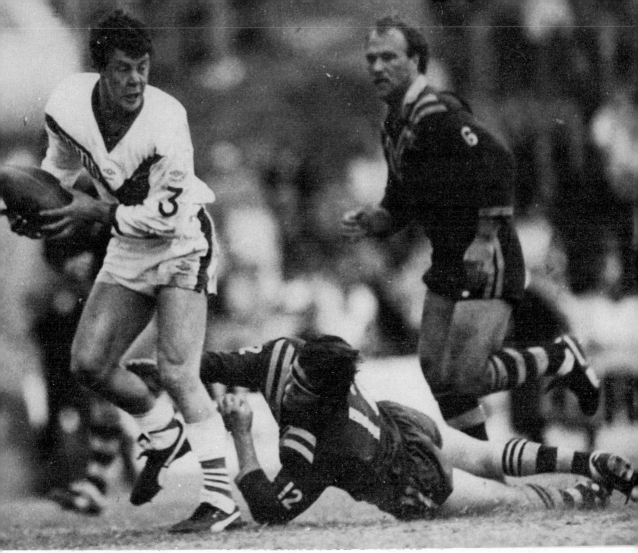

9. The impressive performances of teenage centre Garry Schofield clearly demonstrated that British Rugby League can look forward to the future with some optimism, particularly if there are more youngsters of his calibre bidding for national honours. His confidence, speed and positional sense were seen in the first Test at Sydney on 9 June when, having beaten the lunging dive of Wayne Pearce, he was trying immediately to open out play to his wing.

Hanley and Smith, but again, defensively, they did not seem to be the answer he was looking for when eight minutes later the Newcastle second-row forward, Mal Graham, took advantage of their indecision. He shot past Hanley, who had been drawn out of position, passed to the hooker, Rex Wright, who, despite a fine recovery tackle from Hanley, still managed to get a pass to his colleague in support, scrum-half Craig Higgins. His try beneath the posts, and the conversion by Elwin, brought the scores level. The Lions were then subjected to enormous pressure for ten minutes as Newcastle launched a series of 'bombs' at Burke who, thankfully, stood solid as rock.

Great tries are often scored when a team is under pressure. However, I am sure that few thought they would see a spectacular effort from Hanley when his scrum-half, Holding, fed the scrum 5 yards from the British line and raced round the blind side. He passed to Hanley, who shrugged off the Newcastle loose forward, Pitman, then handed off the cover scrum-half, Higgins, before racing 95 yards to the try-line where, after rounding full-back Elwin, he placed the ball in the corner. It was a magnificent effort, to be complemented by a powerful touchline conversion from Mick Burke.

At half-time, the score was 18–12 to the Lions, and the game was as good as over. Well, not quite, because as a result of the retirement of the prop forward, Lee Crooks, to be replaced by Harry Pinner – a move which meant David Hobbs moving to prop – Britain now experienced difficulty in the scrums. With skipper Brian Noble outhooked by five scrums to nil, and with Britain repeatedly penalized for offences at the play-the-ball, usually for not facing straight at the opposition, Newcastle attacked throughout the second half, frequently retaining possession for as many as thirty tackles at a time. However, Britain's defence held firm, thanks mainly to try-saving tackles at full-back by Burke, and Newcastle were able to score only once. In contrast, a brilliant solo effort from Neil Holding, in which he twice kicked ahead over a distance of 70 yards, and a slick handling effort from Pinner, Holding, Schofield and Hanley, before winger Clark scored, saw Britain ease out comfortably to a sound win. (**Final score: Newcastle 18   Great Britain 28.**)

The game had not been a convincing win for Britain in their final match prior to the first Test, but at least the defensive strategy had again been tested and found to be in good order, while the pace and flair of Holding and Hanley showed that the team did have try-scoring potential from anywhere on the field if only it could match the Australians in the forwards.

The game also presented Ron Barritt with more injury problems – a hip injury to Lee Crooks, stitches to the head for David Hobbs and a bad knock on the right wrist of Oldham's Mick Worrall. These injuries, coupled with the news that the Widnes pair, Gregory and Lydon, would not be available for Test selection because of shoulder bruising and Achilles tendon trouble respectively, forced Myler to name this squad of eighteen players on the Monday morning before the big game: Burke, Drummond, Foy, Schofield, Mumby, Hanley, Holding, Joyner, Donlan, Worrall, Rayne, Noble, Goodway, Adams, Crooks, Hobbs, Burton and Beardmore. With the team undefeated after six matches and with the whole party in confident spirits, the stage was set.

First Test
Sydney, 9 June
Australia 25   Great Britain 8

The atmosphere in Sydney before a Rugby League Test, intensified by the Sydney newspapers, whose correspondents seem to compete in pouring out their invective on the luckless 'Poms', is more than usually frenetic. Yet as the week wore on there was a noticeable shift in favour of Britain's prospects after the sarcasm of the early days of the tour. Originally labelled 'the Milky Bar kids' and 'the Pygmies', the British squad so impressed the Australian press with their constructive and punishing training schedule that the mood changed, with one important observer remarking: 'Don't get carried away with this "fresh faced kids" image, this side can win!'

The squad was a young one, with an average age of only 24, and on the Monday, Tuesday and Wednesday of the week prior to the first Test they showed all the virtues of youth in their training. Ambition and determination were obvious, as virtually all the squad endured twice-daily sessions, with the emphasis in the mornings on the physical, and in the afternoons on the tactical, aspects of the match.

Injuries still prevailed in the camp, with the result that in addition to Gregory and Lydon, Rayne, Holding, Crooks and Joyner spent three days under the care of Ron Barritt away from the glare of the Australian media. Intensive treatment at a city gymnasium meant that by Wednesday evening all save John Joyner, whose pulled hamstring still caused him trouble, were pronounced fit. With injury doubts now cleared, Frank Myler was able to name his Test side. And he was also able to take the team away for a full day's tactical preparation at the North Sydney ground before completing preparations with a light session on the Friday.

The announcement of both teams provoked considerable discussion. The axing of Australian players of the calibre of Eric Grothe, Mal Meninga and Peter Sterling, all of whom had been stars in the 1982 series, aroused considerable hostility throughout Australia. With the selection of the Australian team delayed until after the annual Queensland v. New South Wales match (the State of Origin match), in which Queensland heavily defeated NSW, deadlock on the selection panel had to be resolved by the Australian Rugby League chairman, Ken Arthurson, amid heated accusations that many of the selections were 'politically motivated and voted upon in relation to the home State of the player or selector'. Whatever the feelings of the Australian public, however, there was relief in the British camp at the omission of some star names. There were also rumours of rivalry in the Australian camp between the nine Queenslanders and the rest, especially as Frank Stanton had been named as coach rather than the Queensland coach, Artie Beetson. Nevertheless, after intensive fitness tests, the team worked under Stanton with its customary vigour, while the coach once again displayed his usual thoroughness by putting on video screenings of the 1982 third Test at Headingley. He restricted the viewing to the first half, when Australia had been held 6–4.

The British selection had been determined more by injury than by good form. With Tony Myler having played only fifty-eight minutes' rugby since arriving in Australia, and with Ron Duane sadly out of the tour, Frank Myler had also to contend with the loss of Joyner and Donlan who aggravated back injuries on the Tuesday. Gregory and Lydon, having been declared unfit on the Monday, made remarkable recoveries to the extent that Lydon, because of his versatility, was named as back substitute. To the surprise of many, there was no place for Gregory, even at stand-off, where there were problems. Instead the coach preferred the 20-year-old Oldham player Des Foy, whose previous four outings had been on the wing and whose only experience of the position had been a brief spell at Oldham with Myler as his coach. Foy himself was confident of facing the Australian skipper Wally Lewis – 'Whoever you are marking at international level you are marking a good player' – while Frank Myler's gamble was one taken in the belief that 'Foy does have pace and is a good footballer. I think he'll do the job.'

Apart from loose forward, where the ball-playing skills of Harry Pinner might have been put to good use, the forwards selected themselves by virtue of their proven defensive qualities on the tour. Whether that defence would hold in the forwards and in midfield, where Garry Schofield became the youngest ever British Test player in Australia, remained to be seen. What did not hold was Myler's luck, for in the last serious training session, held in secret at North Sydney on the Thursday, Keith Rayne, the rugged Leeds prop, broke down even though his knee bruising was thought to have improved. The resulting forward reshuffle meant Andy Goodway moving up to the prop position.

Despite the first cool, overcast day in Sydney for two weeks, a good-sized crowd turned up to watch this the first Test match in the thirty-second series between these old adversaries, and greeted the slow walk on to the field by the 1984 Lions with the traditional boos reserved for visitors at the Cricket Ground. Yet the British were not without support as Union Jacks were raised aloft on the 'hill' and a corporal in ceremonial uniform from the 1st battalion, the Green Howards, strode towards the two assembled teams. His uniform contrasted sharply with the suit of John Brown, the Australian Minister for Sport, who welcomed the players on to the pitch prior to the national anthems, played in respectful silence.

The silence did not last for long. The match erupted in a brawl in the fourth minute following the first scrum, when Brown and Crooks, the two props, burst from the mêlée swinging punches at each other. The trouble soon spread, with Goodway heavily involved and with scrum-half Holding receiving some nasty treatment from a couple of Australians as he was lying on the floor. Whatever the cause, whether it was the fact that the Australians were too 'psyched up' following their visit to see Charles Bronson in the film *The Evil that Men Do* the previous evening, or whether it was the determination of the young British pack to assert themselves early, matters soon cooled down under the referee, Ray Shrimpton. Test matches have a history of early flare-ups, but the fisticuffs are soon forgotten once the players' manliness has been proved.

Frank Myler's ploy of using the two wings, Drummond and Hanley, as runners in midfield proved effective in the early stages of the game. Their entry into the line between the centres caused problems for Australia, as did strong drives from Burton and Goodway in the forwards. Such early pressure was rewarded with a penalty to Britain 25 yards out as Australia strayed offside in an effort to restrain an attack. Unfortunately, Burke missed the kick at goal and was therefore unable to give Britain the boost of an early 2 points lead. The Australian winger, Conlon, made no such mistake in the twelfth minute, when he was presented with a similar opportunity for a similar offence.

The opening twenty minutes had seen both sides tackling fiercely, the play moving from end to end only by kicking, with the intention of breaking up the strong defensive cover of both teams. One long, relieving 60-yard kick by full-back Burke, and a short chip kick through the Australian cover by Holding, helped to turn the Australian defence, but neither player was able to match the pressure exerted on the British defence by the Australian stand-off Lewis. His high 'bombs' were especially dangerous and were only taken with the greatest bravery by Burke, who needed every ounce of his huge bulk to fend off would-be chasers and tacklers as he leaped for the descending ball. It was while covering one of these 'bombs' in the twentieth minute that Britain suffered the cruel blow of losing Holding and, possibly, the first Test.

Scrum-half Holding, who had been worrying the stronger but slower Australian scrum-half, Murray, with his darting runs from the scrum and play-the-balls, was caught 5 yards from his line by Boustead, after fielding yet another Lewis kick, and was left writhing in agony, unable to play the ball. Despite prompt attention from Ron Barritt, Holding was forced to leave the field with strained ligaments in the left knee. His absence was crucial. In the one-minute delay before the substitute, Joe Lydon, was allowed on the field, the Australian captain, Wally Lewis, sensing Britain's disarray at the play-the-

10.   Neil Holding, the Lions' scrum-half, wears an anguished expression as he is led from the field in the first Test by David Hobbs (left) and physiotherapist Ron Barritt. Holding's injury to knee ligaments had serious consequences in this Test, as it allowed the Australian pairing of Murray and Lewis to dominate the match from the half-back position.

ball without Holding, moved to first receiver to take the ball 15 yards out from the British line. He cut inside the first attempted tackle, passed to the speedy second-row forward Pearce, who was stopped 2 yards from the line by Burke. With Burke unable to put Pearce to the ground, it was the simplest of movements for Lewis to back up his colleague, accept a further pass and score beneath the posts.

Lewis's try gave Conlon the easiest of conversions to make the score 8–0 to Australia. The try, while Britain were down to twelve men, was costly, but the loss of Holding was to have the biggest bearing on the result. Despite the effort and tenacity of young Schofield, who moved to scrum-half, Britain no longer had a half-back capable of weaving, dodging and making play from the scrums or play-the-balls. There was no player to put pressure on the Australian defence by taking the ball up to them before off-loading to supporting forwards. Only Adams at loose forward was left for that role. Of the midfield backs, there were three wingers-cum-centres in Foy, Schofield and Lydon, all of whom were more used to running off people than creating play. The other, Mumby, was a regular full-back, more experienced in linking into play than creating it in midfield. The piercing, darting runs and the aggression usually associated with half-back play were now lost, and this was to prove costly.

The remaining twenty minutes of the first half saw some strong forward play from the prop Goodway and the second-row forward Burton, but their bursts were invariably held by the strong tackling of Price, Pearce and Niebling in the back three of the Australian pack. The main threat from the Lions came in two jinking runs from Foy and Schofield, but neither could race fully clear of the cover. At the same time, Britain's wingers, Hanley and Drummond, whether sidestepping in midfield or, as with Hanley in one race down the left wing, with sheer strength allied to pace, caused panic in the Australian ranks. Sadly, the Lions' pressure brought only 2 points from Burke's boot five minutes before the half-time whistle, but they had only themselves to blame.

By dropping too many passes and by kicking badly, the Lions had been unable to maintain full pressure in the Australian 25-yard area beyond three or four tackles. Many kicks were too deep – giving the new Australian full-back, Gary Jack, plenty of time to retrieve the ball and gain ground – or they went straight to touch on the full, bringing a scrum where the ball had been originally kicked. And whenever a 'bomb' was put up on the full-back or wings the British players rarely raced up to challenge the catcher with the speed that marked the Australians.

However, there had been little variety from the Australian forwards, held in a vice-like grip by skipper Noble and his men; throughout it was Lewis who proved the inspiration of his side. His kicking, whether deep or short, sent Britain scuttling back in defence, and his wide passing gave plenty of room to

11. The inability of the Lions always to dump the opposition in the tackle meant that only too often the ball was swept out to other players running in support. Here, in the first Test, the Australian prop Dave Brown cleverly manages to pass the ball despite Chris Burton's solid drive into his chest and Brian Noble's fearless tackle round his ankles.

his centres, Kenny and Miles, who were stopped only by the solid tackling of Mumby and Schofield. The pressure exerted by Lewis, invariably at first receiver at the play-the-balls, meant that the British forwards could rarely leave him to cover out wide, as they never knew whether he would run himself, pass or kick. This was the problem for Britain. Lacking a creative half-back, Mick Adams was responsible for moving the ball from first receiver; in this role he was too predictable and lacked the pace of Lewis to create much trouble in

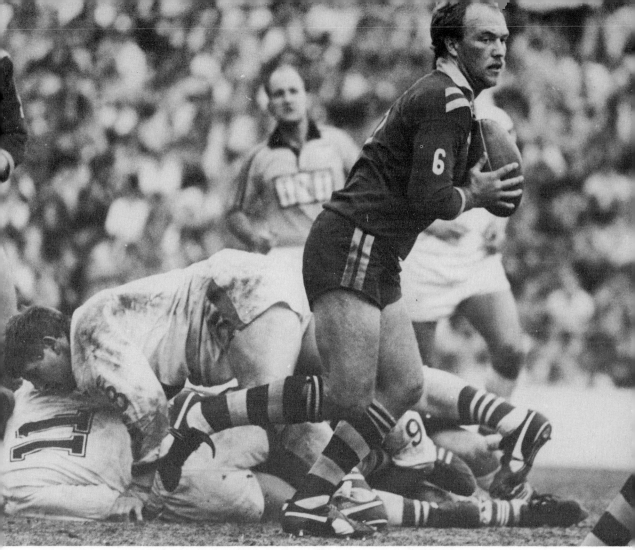

12. Lewis's ability to set up an assortment of plays from set pieces was clearly demonstrated in all the Tests. Here, in the first Test match, with the Lion's pack in a heap on the ground, Lewis sets off to launch his three-quarters on yet another attack.

the Kangaroos' defence. Because of this, skipper Noble himself was forced to dart away from the acting half-back position to relieve pressure on his attacking line on three or four occasions. Nevertheless, the first half had rekindled the fire and enthusiasm lacking in the previous two series, and none could doubt the fitness, determination and positive attitude of this Great Britain side.

The opening ten minutes of the second half saw Britain subjected to the most intense pressure on their line, with centre Keith Mumby and Garry Schofield having to stop Miles and Kenny in full flight for the try-line. It was a testimony to the defensive qualities of this Lions' side that the tackling of Crooks, Noble, Goodway and others was so effective that Australia, again through skipper Lewis, had to resort to aerial 'bombs' to force a try. Burke and Drummond had both fielded Lewis's kicks brilliantly before poor Ellery Hanley misjudged a high swirling ball beneath his posts. In contrast to the British side, Murray, the Australian scrum-half, followed up quickly, seized the ball and, following a quick play-the-ball before Britain could recover, Pearce and Kenny swept the ball out wide to the loose forward, Ray Price, who dummied his way over to score in the fiftieth minute. With the score at 12–2 to Australia and thirty minutes to play, everyone wondered whether, as in the previous two series, the floodgates would open to reveal Britain's old deficiencies. Not so, for under their tireless captain, Brian Noble, the team resurrected some old-fashioned 'British bulldog' spirit to hit back hard.

The journalists in the press box stood to applaud when, following a brief fracas from which Crooks and Dowling were despatched to the sin-bin for ten minutes, Britain's flying wing, Des Drummond, gave a glimpse of his talents. Receiving the ball from Lydon, about 45 yards from the Australian line, and seemingly hemmed in on the touchline, Drummond chose to cut inside. In a marvellous exhibition of pace, balance and swerve he made his way round Pearce, Niebling, Price and Lewis before delivering a perfectly timed pass as he half rounded the full-back Jack. Garry Schofield had timed his run to perfection and had only to retain the ball to score beneath the posts, thereby giving Burke the easiest of conversions. The Union Jacks fluttered, a few Australian heads dropped and, for the first time in six years, the fight for the Ashes was no foregone conclusion.

Great Britain hit hard with runs from wings Hanley and Drummond, and Foy raised hopes with a jinking midfield run, but the final twenty minutes were to illustrate once more the lack of a true half-back in the British team. Again it was Lewis who brought Australia to life. Having made a try for Boustead, who had received from Kenny, using his speed and swerve to round Goodway, Lewis calmly dropped a goal from close range. The game was sealed two minutes before time when Murray, from 25 yards out, darted from the base of the scrum between Adams and Schofield to score. Yet Britain had not lacked fire; perhaps they had too much when the substitute, Hobbs, felled the Australian hooker, Conescu, with a foul elbow tackle. This incident, which resulted in the hooker being carried off on a stretcher and Hobbs being sent off in the last seconds of the match, proved the only unsavoury note in a Test match which had roused the interest of all at the Cricket Ground.

The Australian players lavished high praise on the British performance, none more so than Brett Kenny, who himself had had a successful tour of

13. When an irresistible force meets an immovable object, who gives way? On this occasion the Lions' defence was unshaken against the grim-faced challenge of the Australian loose forward Ray Price in the first Test match at Sydney.

Britain in 1982. And coach Frank Stanton declared the British team to be 'the best British side I have coached against'. Britain had at last matched the Australians for fitness, pride and effort. Their three-quarters had displayed traditional British skills but were still inferior to an Australian side which rarely rose to great heights. The Lions' kicking was ineffective and misdirected; their play round the play-the-balls was too static; and, despite Herculean efforts from the forwards, they lacked true pace in the pack. In truth, such was the control which the Australian captain, Wally Lewis, exerted on the game that if he had changed sides, Great Britain might have won instead of being defeated 8–25.

Australia: Jack (Balmain, Sydney); Boustead (Manly, Sydney), Miles (Wynnum-Manly, Brisbane), Kenny (Parramatta, Sydney), Conlon (Canterbury, Sydney); Lewis (Wynnum-Manly, Brisbane) captain, Murray (Redcliffe, Brisbane); Brown (Manly, Sydney), Conescu (Gladstone, Brisbane), Dowling (Wynnum-Manly, Brisbane), Niebling (Redcliffe, Brisbane), Pearce (Balmain, Sydney), Price (Parramatta, Sydney)

Substitutes: Young (St George, Sydney) for Brown after 68 minutes, Close (Manly, Sydney) not used

Scorers: tries – Price, Lewis, Boustead, Murray; goals – Conlon (4); drop goal – Lewis

Great Britain: Burke (Widnes); Drummond (Leigh), Schofield (Hull), Mumby (Bradford Northern), Hanley (Bradford Northern); Foy (Oldham), Holding (St Helens); Crooks (Hull KR), Noble (Bradford Northern) captain, Goodway (Oldham), Burton (Hull KR), Worrall (Oldham), Adams (Widnes)

Substitutes: Lydon (Widnes) for Holding after 23 minutes, Hobbs (Featherstone Rovers) for Crooks after 72 minutes

Scorers: try – Schofield; goals – Burke (2)

Referee: R. Shrimpton (New Zealand)

Attendance: 30,190

5

THE LIONS IN AUSTRALIA: TO THE SECOND AND THIRD TESTS

Lewis would have to be contained if success was to be gained in the second Test and it was to Queensland, his home state, that the Lions journeyed next. If they were to find a team to level the series it would be in the matches to be played during the next two weeks along the coast of the Barrier Reef. With Neil Holding detained in hospital in Sydney, where it was feared that torn ligaments in his left knee might dash any further tour hopes, and with the Warrington centre, Ron Duane, about to return home, Frank Myler flew to Bundaberg knowing that any hope of success must depend on a rejuvenated Gregory and the return to fitness of his Widnes partner, Tony Myler.

Though David Hobbs received a suspension of three matches and a fine of £700 at a hastily convened judiciary meeting for his offence in the first Test, the problems surrounding the half-backs were to dominate the next two games. There was relief in the British camp when Holding rejoined them from hospital in Sydney, by a special flight, on the Monday of the fixture against Wide Bay. With the news that the injury was not as bad as was feared and that, after a little of his cartilage had been removed and with daily treatment, he would be ready for training in a couple of weeks, Holding once more became his cheerful self. But the person who needed to have his spirits raised was his stand-off partner, Tony Myler, who, despite strenuous efforts to build up his suspect knee, was still enduring considerable pain. The Lions' management thus had the player who had made the scrum-half Test position his own, Neil Holding, and the player who had been expected to secure the stand-off position, Tony Myler, both in difficulties. For Myler, aided by pain-killing injections to the knee during the matches, the next 160 minutes of play in Queensland were crucial. For Andy Gregory, his Widnes half-back partner, this was an opportunity to win back his coveted Great Britain scrum-half place.

The match against Wide Bay was played at Bundaberg on 11 June, a public

14.   Ellery Hanley's powerful dive for the line to score against Wide Bay at Bundaberg on 11 June was just one of those exciting bursts of inspired play which had spectators roaring with approval.

holiday to celebrate the Queen's birthday. Whether the carnival atmosphere at the Salter Oval, where children played alongside the touchlines and spectators sat in cars behind the white palings surrounding the cricket outfield, contributed to the casual attitude of the Great Britain team is debatable. What is not in question is the contribution of the referee, Mick Hourigan. Even the Australians packed into the tiny grandstand which skirted the cricket boundary were upset at his constant whistling, despite the fact that the penalties were 22–7 in Wide Bay's favour. Although Mr Hourigan, on the advice of manager Dick Gemmell, changed his jersey after twenty minutes to one of a different colour from the home side, it did not affect his insistence on stopping the flow of the game at every opportunity.

The resulting hesitancy around the play-the-balls meant that Britain could not develop a pattern to their play despite five tries from Hanley, Beardmore, Basnett, Worrall and Proctor and four goals from Lydon. The tries were, for the most part, individual attempts, and it was only in the sixty-eighth minute that the spectators were treated to the type of support play expected of a national team. Forwards Proctor, Worrall and Case combined well over 50 yards, following scrum-half Gregory's initial break, before Worrall scored his first try of the tour. Frank Myler lambasted the referee for his handling of the match: 'If the referee won't let football be played, then what's the use in coming up here?' He was, however, pleased at the industry, throughout the game, of Beardmore and Case in the pack, and somewhat relieved to see Gregory eager to seize his opportunity and also Tony Myler emerge unscathed after his substitution in the second half. Gregory had looked his usual ebullient self, probing in midfield and distributing passes or kicking with an accuracy that brought tries for Proctor and Basnett. Tony Myler, with his knee heavily strapped and with a wasted look to the thigh above, played with his customary energy, made a couple of clean breaks and gained in confidence as the game wore on.

The gloom surrounding the half-back prospects had lifted somewhat, but the tries scored by the tall, gangling centre Gorman and the diminutive scrum-half Ovens for Wide Bay, both stemming from weaving runs in midfield, further illustrated the lack of depth in the backs in the tour party capable of resisting strong pressure. Nevertheless, the Lions had shown the ability to score entertaining tries. (**Final score: Wide Bay 18   Great Britain 28.**)

Bundaberg, situated on Australia's 'sunshine coast' and noted more for its pioneer aviator Bert Hinkler than for its rugby, reserved its worst weather of the winter for the British party's stay. Hardly cheered by news of a mini-heatwave in Britain, the players spent three days in their beautiful beach hotel watching the rain through the large glass windows of the lounge. Some, like Garry Schofield, Steve Donlon, Brian Case, Andy Gregory and Keith Mumby, sought relief out at sea and headed for the Great Barrier Reef in a yacht, only to be turned back at the harbour mouth because of high winds – shades of Blackpool on a summer's day! Others, like Des Foy, tried their hand at cooking on the hotel's mini-grills. Specializing in 'whole chicken roasts', Foy soon had a willing customer in his room-mate Ray Ashton who acquired a taste for chicken which was to last him throughout the tour. Despite the assurances of Mick Adams that hot weather could be expected in Queensland, the players agreed with him only when, on touching down at Rockhampton, the next stop, where they were due to play Central Queensland, the sun was high in the sky.

Spirits in the touring party continued high, and nowhere was this more evident than at training on the afternoon before the match. Anyone watching the two-hour session, only hours after the flight from Bundaberg, must have been left with the feeling that the opposition was in for some rough treatment. On the field at the Rockhampton club, the players went through their physical routines under Rod McKenzie with great relish, amusing the onlookers by breaking into song as they raced round the perimeter in two single-file groups, each chorus competing with the other. Following that session, under the guidance of Frank Myler, the team to face Central Queensland worked at moves which would give variety round the play-the-balls and practised forward runs off Gregory's short passes. Attention was given to kick-offs and retrieving lost balls, while much work was also done with long clearance kicks upfield, some of which interfered with the progress of the injured Crooks and Holding as they ran round the pitch. Both Crooks and Holding were running at various speeds, trying out their respective leg injuries and reporting at intervals for advice and treatment from Ron Barritt, who had set up his clinic at the corner of the pitch. Dispensing potions and liniment from his bag, he carried out running repairs as players left training at frequent intervals. Manager Dick Gemmell liaised with the local press and, in his usual diplomatic style, managed to 'tell them everything without really saying anything'. He attended to the Central Queensland officials and checked on arrangements for the following evening. Perhaps the most vital cog in the well-oiled machinery was the small figure of the business manager, Roland Davis, who accompanied me on a tour of the ground.

Greeted by Rockhampton's president and the news that he anticipated gate receipts 'of about A$7,500', Roland showed his steel with the reply: 'In which case this will be the last time a Great Britain touring party will be visiting Central Queensland.' Taken aback by the reply, but amused by the honesty, the president allowed Davis and me to check all the turnstiles and their telltale 'clicker numbers', and to view the fence where 'people often climb over'. But no one tried this when Davis stationed four burly British forwards alongside the fence. The final sight of him counting the seats in the grandstand was proof that, like the score, the returned receipts would be higher than anyone in Rockhampton had anticipated. And they were. At about A$22,000 they were far in excess of the earlier estimate.

The match attracted 5,600 spectators, the biggest crowd to watch a touring side for fourteen years. The floodlit pitch at Browne Park was the only empty space as supporters searched frantically for a vantage point. Children poured over the boundary wall; adults sat in trees; and many even invaded the press box where the media ranks were suddenly swelled to fifty or sixty – David Brook, chairman of MMP, the sponsors of the tour, who too had sought refuge in

72

the box, was left hanging from a perch at the back like a pigeon about to leave its loft.

But, wherever one sat, the lasting impression of the game will surely be the sight of young Garry Schofield racing through the ranks of Central Queensland for one of his four tries. With five goals as well he notched a personal points tally of 26 and thrilled the crowd with his pace and sense of timing. From the twelfth minute when, following a short burst by Gregory, he raced on to a pass from Burke to leave defenders trailing in a 40-yard sprint to the line, his anticipation proved uncanny in one so young. His hat-trick of tries in the second half all revealed his ability to read play and be at the side of the ball carrier whenever a movement appeared to break down.

In the forty-eighth minute he appeared alongside hooker Noble, who had broken from the acting half-back position, and raced 30 yards to score beneath the posts. Fifteen minutes later he followed a good break by prop Keith Rayne and was able to complete the last 50 yards when Rayne passed out of the tackle. He completed his tries ten minutes before time with another 40-yard run, following a chip kick by Tony Myler and a neat pass from his co-centre Keith Mumby. Opportunism at its best! Keith Mumby, looking faster than I have ever known him and scoring a try himself through determined running along the left wing, and Garry Schofield were the key figures in this heavy defeat of an outclassed Central Queensland side. Hanley and Drummond again provided speed and thrust on the wings, their frequent incursions into midfield causing panic in the opposition ranks. Change of pace, especially from Drummond when he beat his opposite winger and the full-back for a try in the corner, often left the defence wrong-footed.

The major interest in the match, from the British point of view, once again centred on the half-backs and loose-forward positions. Myler's scrum-half partner, Andy Gregory, provided him with good service, and both distributed the ball out wide to the three-quarters. Under instructions from the coach, Gregory was trying to stand much deeper when in possession in order to create time and space for his forwards before the inevitable tackling barrier which Australian sides quickly create. Before retiring injured, he produced the gaps in the first half for Burton, Noble and Goodway to exploit. He also allowed his partner, Myler, the room to link with the centres, which he did to good effect. Myler provided a sound link and frequently appeared further out on the flanks to keep the ball moving, all of which helped him to gain in confidence. Still in some discomfort from his knee, it was ironic that he should receive a knock on the thigh of the other leg that caused him to miss the next game.

As loose forward Flanagan was unfit with a bruised shoulder, as Pinner was still carrying a bruised hip injury from the game at Bundaberg, and as Adams

15.   Prop Mike O'Neill shows a surprising turn of speed against Wide Bay at Bundaberg on 11 June, leaving the cover floundering as he races through the defence with hooker Kevin Beardmore in close support.

was rested on the substitutes' bench, Mick Worrall was selected at loose forward as an experiment, with mixed results. Playing his usual strong tackling game, he was hardly the ideal man to be thrust into the ball-handling role at first receiver. His knowledge of defence at the base of the scrum was also called in question when he was twice beaten on the blind-side by Central Queensland's lively scrum-half, Geoff Hunt. His spirit was not in doubt, however, when the experiment was halted at half-time with the usual loose forward, Adams, taking his place. Mick was later found to be suffering from a severe abscess in the mouth which, despite treatment, caused him to miss the next two matches. (**Final score: Central Queensland 12   Great Britain 44.**)

At this stage of the tour it was heartening to know that crowds were now being attracted by the quality of the Lions' play. Nowhere was this more evident than in the third match along the 'sunshine coast' against Northern Queensland at Townsville on 17 June.

Mick Adams's prediction of sunshine had indeed come true at Townsville, and the players, whether swimming or climbing the surrounding trees for coconuts, were able to relax their bruised limbs. For Mick Burke, with a bruised shoulder, Chris Burton, with rib damage, and Steve Donlon, still troubled by his back injury, the sun was to prove the healer; for others it was the setting for enjoyment off the field. By day Neil Holding entertained the British party with his barking-dog impressions in the hotel pool, almost winning applause from ice-dance champions Torvill and Dean, resting at the same hotel during their own tour of Australia. By night, beneath the palm trees of the open air restaurant, the order was for T-bone steaks, rump steaks, carpet-bag steaks, pepper steaks and more steaks, save for Oldham's Ray Ashton, who kept to his chicken on the advice of room-mate and personal chef, Des Foy.

The casual traveller may enjoy sun, sea and sand, but idyllic conditions are no friend of Rugby League players when the temperature is 86°F just five minutes before kick-off, even at Townsville, one of the most picturesque grounds in the world. From the press box the sight of Magnetic Island, set in a shimmering blue sea, lapping gently on to the palm-fringed sands, is hardly conducive to a commentator more used to reporting matches from Runcorn or Widnes. Nor were 6,000 dry Australians, clutching beer cans and thronging the tiny arena, a particularly friendly sight for the British players emerging from the tunnel. And yet, after the victory over North Queensland, who were expected to be the strongest country opposition, those very supporters were thirsting for more British rugby!

Whatever the shortcomings of the party as a whole, the tour was certainly creating the personalities the Australian spectators wanted to see and, although this victory was essentially a team effort, the name of Hanley was on everyone's lips. In mastering the intense heat, the forwards, especially O'Neill, Crooks and Case, all three prop forwards at home, had shown the value of their harsh training programme. Des Drummond again displayed his pace in scoring two tries; and the combination of Ray Ashton, at scrum-half, and Harry Pinner, at loose forward, provided the ball distribution leading to another seven tries.

It was Hanley, though, who caught the spectators' imagination. His display of strength, as he bumped off one would-be tackler after another, had the crowd roaring, particularly when he scored his second try of the match. Catching the ball from the kick-off, loose forward Pinner passed to Drummond, who drove his small but compact frame at a cluster of North Queensland tacklers, and

16. Good 'little 'uns' confront each other! A determined Andy Gregory, the Lions' scrum-half, threatens to run through his opposite number, Ovens, of Wide Bay, in the match at Bundaberg on 11 June.

burst through at the other side. After sprinting 40 yards, he transferred the ball to Hanley, who appeared by his side from the wing. Hanley's pace held off the attentions of the Queensland wing, Shearer, while he crashed through the tackle of full-back Brunker by strength alone. Such tries, and his involvement in others, were sufficient for him to receive a standing ovation from the fiercely partisan Townsville crowd as he left the field, to be substituted by Des Foy in the sixty-seventh minute. As with the Wigan crowd who applauded a passing movement of the Australians in the second Test in 1982, here at Townsville the reverse was happening. As Hanley waved to the crowd in appreciation, he had gained the ultimate accolade which is only rarely bestowed by your opponents' fans, especially when their team has been so comprehensively beaten.

And they had been well beaten, for despite four tries against them, the British side had again displayed an ability to score exciting tries from long range. The recurring problem, however, was their inability to endure too much attacking pressure close to their line. Two tries to the Queensland forwards, Colwell and Morrissey, who had plunged over the line from 5 yards, showed that the British forwards were still not moving up fast enough at the play-the-ball when near the try-line. Such tries, as in all three of these Queensland country games, were responsible for keeping pressure on the Lions and never allowing the team to win with the margins it should have done. (**Final score: North Queensland 20   Great Britain 38.**)

These games on the coast of Queensland had put the party in good heart for the flight to Brisbane and a stay of thirteen days in that beautiful city astride the Brisbane river. The strains of 'High Hopes', 'Running Bear' and 'Abide With Me' added to any anxiety the passengers might have had as the plane from Townsville cruised high at 27,000 feet amid intermittent cloud. Any fear of flying, though, was forgotten as the whole squad accompanied the air hostess in her safety routine, mimicking her actions, repeating her words and reducing her to fits of laughter as she grappled with the emergency oxygen mask. Few expected that the first game they would play away from their new base at Too-woomba would produce their first defeat in games outside the Tests, and the first jolt to morale.

The precedent for defeat had been set in 1979, when Toowoomba had beaten the Lions of that year. In 1984 the supporters who had travelled out in large parties from Britain, and who awaited the arrival of the British team at the ground, were deeply disappointed by the inept performance of their side. On a chilly, overcast day the only things to warm the British supporters were the meat pies.

In making his selection for the match, Frank Myler felt he could not risk any of his potential Test players. Knowing that in the squad of thirty he had only sixteen or seventeen men really capable of matching the Australians in Test football, he was worried about possible injuries. Never before on the tour had all the Test 'certainties' been left out, either by injury or design. On this occasion Myler omitted them and had to accept, in the defeat that followed, that many of his players were not yet ready for the demands of the tour.

The defeat by Toowoomba was not as close as the score might suggest, for the tourists trailed badly throughout the match, having taken the lead after only five minutes through a John Basnett try. Toowoomba gave the appearance of being a very mediocre team when scrum-half Andy Gregory swept through their ranks and slipped the ball to prop Mike O'Neill, who promptly passed to

17. Wide Bay's defence is clinically dissected by Great Britain's Tony Myler as he makes a classic stand-off break.

Steve Donlon, playing in the unusual role of full-back. Donlan's speed and Basnett's strength did the rest in scoring the first try wide out on the left wing. Such a try should have heralded a points onslaught from Britain, and the British supporters, having devoured their mountain of meat pies, sat back for the exhibition. They were, however, treated to a woeful display in which, once again, a paper-thin defence on the flanks allowed Toowoomba to race into a 12–4 half-time lead through tries by centre Coutts and loose forward Stains, who did little more than charge at the opposition. The Lions' defence crumbled through feeble tackling.

Though winger Garry Clark hit back with a 35-yard interception try within four minutes of the resumption, and Featherstone's second-row forward, David

Hobbs, kicked a penalty goal two minutes later, Britain continued to beat themselves. Apart from the two prop forwards, Brian Case and Mike O'Neill, both of whom had energetic games, few in the pack ran from any depth, and they failed to link with the ball carrier. They preferred to stand as if mesmerized by Toowoomba's keen tackling. Nor did the backs have any heart for attacking. Instead they frittered away chances with fumbles, lost balls and too much sideways running against a defence which contained many gaps in the centre.

The match-winning try, scored by Toowoomba's winger Steve Gibson in the fifty-ninth minute, illustrated amply the lack of cohesion and mostly aimless running in Great Britain's play. At 12–10 to Toowoomba, and sensing that Toowoomba could easily be overhauled, Britain finally mounted an enterprising attack. After a strong plunge from Mike O'Neill down the left flank, in which he took play to the home side's 25-yard area, the ball was quickly transferred to the right where a simple overlap existed. A score would have been a formality. However, poor Andy Gregory, having a nightmare of a match, chose to miss out two players with a pass to the wing, Garry Clark. Unfortunately, the ball did not carry; the Toowoomba centre Greg Milne picked it up and sped 50 yards downfield. Although overhauled by Steve Donlan, he was able to pass to his wing, Gibson, for the easiest of tries beneath the posts and a win for Toowoomba, richly deserved. A try by the British centre, Mike Smith, converted by David Hobbs, gave some respectability to the score-line. Frank Myler blasted his side and conceded: 'When you play that badly, you can't expect to win. We will have to do a lot better if we hope to hold Australia in the second Test.' (**Final score: Toowoomba 18   Great Britain 16.**)

Chastened but not too demoralized, the players travelled back to Brisbane in determined mood for the second Test. Skipper Brian Noble, who had not played in the defeat at Toowoomba, once again illustrated his qualities as captain in restoring the team's morale, urging all to give everything in training. With six training sessions, as well as the regular 7.00 a.m. 5-mile run, planned for the four days prior to the Test, manager Dick Gemmell further added to the players' Spartan existence by placing an 11.00 p.m. curfew on the whole party. The training and the curfew were welcomed by all if they would help to beat the Kangaroos at Lang Park. With forwards Harry Pinner and Chris Burton confined to bed on the Wednesday and Thursday prior to the Test, suffering from a mild dose of flu – and their bedroom boldly marked 'unclean' – Frank Myler was unable to name his side until the final work-out on the Saturday morning before the match.

Uppermost in the coach's mind was the need for pace and strength at half-back, the crucial area where Britain had been defeated in the first Test at Sydney. Mick Burke and the three-quarter line had more than matched the Australians and had proved their try-scoring potential throughout the country games. The pack had shared the honours with the Kangaroo forwards, but, at half-back, the Lions had been decisively beaten. In the matches following the first Test, Myler's experiments with that position, in view of the enforced absence of Holding and the careful nursing of stand-off Tony Myler, had not been too successful. The situation was such that, with Holding making a rapid recovery and with Tony Myler able to play, aided by injections to the knee, there was little option left to Frank Myler but to gamble with their inclusion. If both players had been discarded, the alternatives for a half-back pairing would have found Britain wanting in the Test.

Many supporters were amazed to hear of a half-back partnership comprising a scrum-half, Neil Holding, who had not played since the first Test, and a stand-off, Tony Myler, who had played less than 200 minutes' rugby in the previous twelve weeks. They were right to be amazed, but it was really the only option open. With any other combination the Australian half-backs, Murray and Lewis, would have been dominant; with Holding and Myler there was at least the chance of a surprise. The selection of the forwards, when Chris Burton was declared fit, was straightforward once the coach had decided that the form of all three contestants for the loose-forward position had not come up to the mark. Oldham's Mick Worrall was therefore placed ahead of Flanagan, Adams and Pinner because of his steadier tackling abilities; indeed, though the pack lacked a forward with true ball-handling skills, all were strong tacklers.

At the Eastern Suburbs' training ground in Brisbane the physical fitness sessions were relaxed a little, and the practices concentrated on the team to face the Australians, much work being done with the ball. A lot of work was also done on play-the-balls, defensive patterns and retrieving the loose ball. Fielding the high 'bombs' too became the order of the day.

The Australians were forced to pull out their vice-captain, Ray Price, who was suffering from an eye infection, but the inclusion of Paul Vautin was not thought to weaken the team. Nor was there any suggestion that the team might be handicapped by including the giant three-quarters, Grothe and Meninga, for Conlon and Kenny. In fact, their inclusion strengthened the team.

**Second Test
Brisbane, 26 June
Australia 18   Great Britain 6**

The only injury scare in either camp in the vital twenty-four hours before kick-off caused some amusement when it was learned that Britain's hard taskmaster, Rod McKenzie, had pulled a calf muscle. His plight helped to lighten the atmosphere as the players waited for the evening kick-off on a day punctuated by a 3.00 p.m. luncheon for all the squad. When on tour an evening kick-off makes for a long, dull day as players physically and mentally prepare for the big event. On this occasion some passed their time reading or writing letters home; some watched the endless array of old films on television in their bedrooms; others strolled in the sun along the river. However they prepared, few can have imagined the atmosphere at Lang Park prior to that 7.35 p.m. kick-off. The State of Queensland had arranged a magnificent spectacle for its visitors.

On that warm evening the bright floodlights lit up the arena, to welcome first Sir John Bjelke Peterson, the Premier of Queensland, then the parade of Queensland Olympic athletes who were to represent Australia in the Los Angeles games in July, followed by the band of the Royal Australian Artillery. The white top coats of the band stood out like a washing-powder advertisement as they paraded beneath the glare of the lights, but it was the brightness of the fireworks which lit up the skies. Red, white and blue, green and gold – a panorama of colour announced the arrival of the sides on the pitch. The Queenslanders even roared when their idol, Wally Lewis, won the toss, as if, aided by divine intervention, he could do no wrong. And indeed Australia could do little wrong in the first half-hour.

Helped by an early four-to-one scrum possession, Australia exerted intense pressure in the Great Britain half during this period. They were restrained from scoring only by the Lions' heroic defence and their own sloppy handling. The opening ten minutes saw play concentrated on the half-way line with neither side able to create an overlap or break through the line of tacklers. Britain's second-row forward, Goodway, with a powerful tackle, had stopped the giant wing Eric Grothe from stepping dangerously inside, and the new Test player Vautin had caused panic when he raced through a Burke tackle. Thankfully, Mick Worrall intercepted his pass to relieve the danger on the British line, but there were few clear chances. Each team sparred as if in the early

81

rounds of a boxing match, looking for weaknesses and probing for openings; seeing none, both turned to kicking the ball. In an effort to gain ground or break up the tight defences both Lewis for Australia and Holding for Britain resorted to chipping the ball to touch or, as in the case of the Australian captain, firing off some of his high 'bombs'. One such 'bomb' was bravely taken by full-back Burke on his own goal-line and with three big Australian forwards bearing down on him.

Once the sides had settled down, both produced the rugby of which they were capable and displayed the two contrasting weapons in their armoury. Britain's pace and footballing skill were shown in the execution of a rare switch in attack in the nineteenth minute, when Tony Myler, from the stand-off position, launched Burke with a long pass to the blind-side of a scrum. Burke, using his bulk to good effect, held off two defenders before transferring the ball to Hanley, well positioned about 15 yards from the try-line. It was a desperate scramble for Australia's lighter wing, Boustead, and the full-back, Gary Jack, to force the British wing into touch at the corner flag.

It was no more desperate, however, than Britain's three-man tackle which stopped left-winger Eric Grothe 5 yards short of the British try-line after Lewis, though well tackled by Burke, had managed to slip out a well-timed pass. Such excitement added to the furore among the fiercely partisan crowd, as forwards Niebling and Rayne fought out a personal duel in the tackles. The temperature rose even higher when the substitute forward, Adams, who had entered the fray in place of Crooks in the eighteenth minute, was involved in a high tackle on Queensland's hero, Wally Lewis. To the amusement of the crowd, on the intervention of the touch judge, Keith Rayne was despatched to the sin-bin to cool off for ten minutes and not the offending Adams. Sadly, ill-tempered duels between Lewis and the British players were to last for the rest of the match, producing a torrid closing ten minutes.

Only a Mal Meninga goal, kicked shortly before Burke failed to equalize with a simple kick which hit the upright, separated the two sides until six minutes before half-time. Britain should then have taken the lead but instead saw Australia's margin increase to 6–0 at the turn round. Despite Rayne's absence, Britain had their best spell of the half, their attacks culminating in the chance of a try which would have rocked the Australians. Tony Myler, coming more into the game as he gained in confidence and pushed his knee injury to the back of his mind, delivered a deft one-handed pass round his opponent to send young-ster Schofield racing clear down the right touchline.

The British supporters jumped to their feet as they sensed a try. Andy Goodway came up alongside Schofield, received his well-timed pass and raced upfield, leaving the Australian cover behind. Unfortunately, his speed took not only the Kangaroos by surprise but even his team mate, Drummond, who had

18.   Australia's Mark Murray was yet another would-be cover tackler left in the wake of Great Britain's elusive winger, Des Drummond, in the second Test at Brisbane on 26 June. With his exciting speed and subtle changes of pace, Drummond came to be recognized by Australian players and spectators alike as a winger of true international class.

hesitated for a second. As a result, the Australian full-back was able to tackle Goodway before Drummond could move alongside, when a try would have been a formality. A similar opportunity, this time to Australia and accepted by them two minutes later, revealed the extra strength of many of their players. Though held in the tackle by three British players, Gene Miles managed to pass the ball to the unmarked Grothe, who merely had to sprint 30 yards to the corner to score. Australia deserved their slender lead. They had accepted their chances, while Britain were still unable to clinch a vital try in the closing seconds of the half. Once again a switch-move, involving Holding, Burke and Hanley, had come to grief 10 yards from Australia's line where, though he looked menacing, the unfortunate Hanley was unable to hold the pass, the ball hitting his right shoulder and rolling to touch.

The first half had been characterized by the strength of the midfield trio of Lewis, Miles and Meninga, who frequently needed the attentions of two or three tacklers to put them to the ground. Loose forward Wayne Pearce had been the only difference between the two packs, his cover tackles effectively destroying any British hopes, and his midfield runs indicating there was worse to come. Burton, Goodway and Noble had borne the brunt of the tackling for Britain, while Britain's extra pace in attack, especially on the right wing where Schofield and Drummond were the equals of any, had exploited what few gaps there were.

The opening ten minutes of the second half gave further proof that Britain really did have try-scoring potential, if only they could eradicate their lapses of concentration when handling or passing. The half-backs, Holding and Myler, combined well after Holding had produced the neatest of chip kicks just outside Britain's 25-yard line. Tony Myler regathered and passed to Schofield in one movement. Schofield, having raced 35 yards downfield, was unable to clinch the try by passing inside to Drummond. Good play by the Australian full-back crowded him towards the touchline, making a pass impossible. Unfortunately, Britain's enterprise could not break down the Australian defence, and Meninga heralded events to come with a further penalty goal, following an offside decision against the loose forward, Mick Worrall. It was strength, allied to pace, which again allowed Australia to dominate, after a shaky spell. Spurred by the sight of their wing, Grothe, fielding a kick deep in his own half and racing across field, swatting away tackles from Mumby, Holding and Goodway, the Australians' pack sprang to life. Pearce, especially, asserted himself, assuming the mantle of the running forward which had first brought his career to prominence in the 1982 series. Receiving the ball to the left of the British goal posts, and thirty yards from the try-line, he suddenly pushed his head back, heaved his chest, galloped through the despairing tackles of Adams and Burton and raced for the line, leaving the gallant Burke trailing on the ground as he touched the ball down. Sheer strength and determination had carried him over. Meninga, too, in the sixty-ninth minute received the ball on the blind side of a scrum from the full-back, Jack, burst through the tackles of Mumby and Myler and scored a try of great strength.

There is no answer to a big man moving at speed, and players like Pearce and Meninga invariably prove the old adage 'a good big 'un will always beat a good little 'un.' But sandwiched between those two Australian efforts, in the best twelve minutes of rugby in the match, was surely proof that 'good little 'uns' with sufficient skill can still outwit others. From inside Great Britain's 25-yard area Myler and Adams combined well to put centre Schofield in the clear, with his wing partner, Drummond, on the outside. Sidestepping and weaving inside, Schofield wrong-footed the cover tacklers and proceeded to inter-pass with Drummond from one side of the field to the other until Goodway linked up in midfield, straightened the movement and gave the ball back to Schofield for the final run-in. Schofield's pace and determined hand-off enabled him to round the wing, Kerry Boustead, to score in the corner. It was a memorable try, covering 80 yards of the pitch, and it fully deserved the conversion which Burke added from the touchline. The crowd appreciated the skills involved, but they did not condone the antics in the final ten minutes when Rayne, Noble, Lewis and Vautin became involved in a series of niggling fouls which resulted in a cheek-bone injury to Vautin, a further five minutes in the sin-bin for Rayne and a broken nose for the captain, Noble. Tempers flared on the British side out of frustration at the manner in which the Australian stand-off, Wally Lewis, was orchestrating events on the field, while Lewis, who felled Noble, was obviously upset at the attempted swipes at his own head. It was regrettable that such a good Test match should degenerate to this level in the closing minutes and provide the Australian press with critical ammunition.

The pre-match favourites Australia fully deserved their victory, but the British team did not deserve the harsh criticism which the press directed at their gallant effort. Comments like 'It's always been part of Great Britain's game that they try to "get" as many players as possible when they know they have lost a match' served only to stir up further trouble in advance of the third Test at Sydney. It was sad to reflect that though Les Boyd, the New South Wales forward, had been rightly banned for a year for indiscriminate use of the elbow at Lang Park a year earlier and the Lions' forward, David Hobbs, had been fined £700 and suspended for three matches for a similar offence in the first Test, Queensland's hero, Wally Lewis, was praised for such an event on television.

As in the first Test, Australia had taken all the chances that came their way and, as many in the British party privately feared, the inclusion of Grothe and Meninga added size and strength to an area in which they were already dominant. Britain's best players – Goodway, Schofield, Drummond and Burton – matched Pearce, Vautin, Lewis and Miles. Britain's forwards had once again endured a fearful battering but had withstood it with the same resolve they had shown in all the major games. The gamble at half-back did not win the match for Britain, but though it was evident on occasions that they were carrying knee injuries, Holding and Myler made a positive contribution to the match, rousing Frank Stanton to comment: 'Playing on one leg they gave us plenty of trouble. What would they be like on two?' The Lions had once again given of their best and were, as Stanton added, 'a real force at international level again'. Yet Australia had still retained the Ashes Trophy and were making preparations for a third win at Sydney in less than two weeks' time.

Australia: Jack (Balmain, Sydney); Boustead (Manly, Sydney), Miles (Wynnum-Manly, Brisbane), Meninga (Souths, Brisbane), Grothe (Parramatta, Sydney); Lewis (Wynnum-Manly, Brisbane) captain, Murray (Redcliffe, Brisbane); Brown (Manly, Sydney), Conescu (Gladstone, Brisbane), Dowling (Wynnum-Manly, Brisbane), Vautin (Manly, Sydney), Niebling (Redcliffe, Brisbane), Pearce (Balmain, Sydney)

Substitutes: Fullerton-Smith (Redcliffe, Brisbane) for Brown after 66 minutes, Mortimer (Canterbury-Bankstown, Sydney) not used

Scorers: tries – Grothe, Pearce, Meninga; goals – Meninga (3)

Great Britain: Burke (Widnes); Drummond (Leigh), Schofield (Hull), Mumby (Bradford Northern), Hanley (Bradford Northern); Myler (Widnes), Holding (St Helens); Rayne (Leeds), Noble (Bradford Northern) captain, Crooks (Hull), Burton (Hull KR), Goodway (Oldham), Worrall (Oldham)

Substitutes: Adams (Widnes) for Crooks after 18 minutes, Gregory (Widnes) for Burke after 71 minutes

Scorers: try – Schofield; goal – Burke

Referee: R. Shrimpton (New Zealand)

Attendance: 26,534

With two fixtures at Tweed Heads and Tamworth before the third Test, Britain were unable to start preparing immediately for the final match in the series to prevent a threatened whitewash. And the problems of a tight schedule were compounded by the list of injuries which made experiments with team selection

19. Always fearless and secure under the high ball, the Lions' full-back Mick Burke also showed in the third Test at Sydney on 7 July that he was prepared to counter-attack with determined runs at the Australian defensive line.

virtually impossible. All this was quietly forgotten by the more vitriolic elements of the Australian press as they criticized the British team for fracturing Paul Vautin's cheekbone and for the knocks Lewis had received in the second Test. They poured scorn on the use of the elbow in the tackle by some of the Lions' forwards and intimated, possibly hopefully, that the third Test would result in a brawl with many of the Australian side seeking retribution. The former Australian star Bobby Fulton even advised the 'Poms' to go home. But few journalists bothered to look at the damage the British players had suffered during the torrid ten minutes at the end of the match at Lang Park. It would have sobered many of them to see Brian Noble return from hospital the next day with a broken nose, Lee Crooks with torn shoulder tendons, Mick Burke nursing bruised ribs and Andy Goodway with a painful arm, all injuries resulting from the previous night's encounter.

The reaction on the day after a defeat in a Test match is always an indication of the resolve of any touring side, and it is to the credit of the 1984 party that they used the following morning's training session largely to restore morale. But luck was still not with them when loose forward Terry Flanagan leaped to catch a high ball, twisted in flight and tore his ankle ligaments. Nor were poor Brian Noble's and Andy Goodway's troubles over. Having contracted a stomach virus, Noble was unable to accompany the party to the holiday resort of Surfers Paradise to rest in the sea and sun before the evening kick-off against Northern Rivers at Tweed Park. And Andy Goodway, who had somewhat similar symptoms, remained in Brisbane for a couple of days with him, acting as the most sympathetic of chambermaids when serving him Lucozade.

British supporters could be forgiven for thinking that the holiday break was continuing when they arrived at Tweed Heads for the Northern Rivers match. Sited next to a new A$12 million entertainments complex, featuring a cinema, three restaurants, lounge bars, a theatre and souvenir shops, and flanked by yachts on the river, the brilliant green of the grass shone beneath the glare of the floodlights as if awaiting a carnival rather than a rugby match. Youngsters wheeled barrows full of steak and sausage round the pitch, the prizes for the raffles at half-time.

Sadly, the carnival atmosphere affected the players' attitude, and they rarely lived up to their potential, relying on individual flashes of brilliance to secure their four tries. Helped by hooker Beardmore's heavy scrum advantage in the first half, the Lions quickly established a 16–2 lead by half-time without playing well. Tries by Clark and Drummond on the wings indicated where the team's strength lay, as both beat three men by sheer speed to score. The third try on the half-hour came as a result of a well-worked run-around forward ploy between Pinner, the captain for the night, and Beardmore, who combined to send David Hobbs crashing for the try-line. These three had too much skill for Northern Rivers, and even after full-back Joe Lydon was sent off for a high tackle four minutes into the second half, the Lions were never in danger of losing.

The loss of Lydon, who had kicked two conversions, gave the opposition vital overlaps in the second half, but their tries only came through the opportunism of their right wing, Gerry O'Neill. His first was the result of intelligent backing up by Judd, while his second came from an alert interception of a pass by Pinner, and he raced 50 yards unopposed. The score had now narrowed to 18–12, David Hobbs having replied with a penalty to the two Northern Rivers converted tries. Then Mike Smith, having moved to stand-off in the closing stages, sealed victory, when, with only six minutes remaining, he dummied his

20. Andy Goodway, another British success on tour, was one of the few players with the strength to drive at and break the tackles of the Australian forwards. He had another fine game in the third Test at Sydney, but the Australian defensive cover was as well organized as ever with Ray Price here standing off to smother the danger should Goodway break through.

way over the line from 25 yards out. David Hobbs, having his best game of the tour, kicked the goal.

The carnival atmosphere had indeed prevailed throughout the match. Little did manager Dick Gemmell realize that the Northern Rivers coach would take him at his word when, before kick-off, they agreed to unlimited substitutions. With Northern Rivers fielding ten substitutes throughout the match, no one was really surprised when at one scrum the referee had to stop play while a seventh forward was removed from the Northern Rivers pack to bring the side down to thirteen men. (**Final score: Northern Rivers 12   Great Britain 24.**)

In defeating Northern Division, New South Wales, in their next match, the Lions were again faced with an abnormal number of substitutions by the opposition. Four fresh players on the field early in the second half no doubt contributed to Northern Division's revival, but their three tries from Carr, Donnelly and Hill resulted more from Britain's casual attitude in defence. The Lions had looked set for an easy win when, following some free-flowing handling movements, they raced ahead to a half-time lead of 18–2. Two tries by Hanley and one from Lydon illustrated the greater pace and skill which the tourists possessed.

Lydon's try in the twenty-first minute came after a ball had been passed at speed through the hands of Adams, Hobbs, Ashton and Myler before the full-back raced into the gap on the right flank to score. Hanley's second try highlighted the pace and opportunism of himself and his wing partner, Drummond, as they combined over 70 yards in beating four covering players. Unfortunately, such skills were forgotten after Smith's try, three minutes after half-time, had given Britain an unassailable lead of 24–2. Sloppy tackling meant defenders were shrugged off at will, while petty infringements in the play-the-balls allowed the opposition eight successive penalties and possession for long stretches. Following a disastrous fifteen-minute spell midway through the second half, when Northern Division narrowed the lead by scoring three tries, with full-back Donnelly converting two of them, Britain recovered with a try by the prop forward, Brian Case. However, few players added to their reputations save the established Test players Hanley and Drummond, who constantly threatened danger, and Case and Hobbs, with their high work-rate, reminded Myler of their bid for Test places. (**Final score: Northern Division 18   Great Britain 32.**)

Third Test
Sydney, 7 July
Australia 20   Great Britain 7

Despite occasional flashes of stylish running, the Lions had not played well in the two games following the second Test and had conceded five tries to mediocre opposition. The tackling in both games had been far too loose and, at times, far too high, allowing tries to be scored from positions close to the try-line by players shrugging off ineffective attempts at a tackle round the shoulders. One factor in losing the second Test had been the high proportion of missed tackles – twenty-two compared with the Australians' six – and the two games since then indicated that this vital aspect of play had not been rectified.

Preparations for the final Test now seemed almost to be jinxed. At the Monday morning training session, following the party's return to Sydney, only eighteen players were able to take the field, faced by a forlorn Frank Myler and a tired Ron Barritt. As if injuries to Schofield, Joyner, Beardmore, Lydon, Flanagan, Rayne, Worrall, Pinner and Goodway were not enough, the squad also contracted a 'flu virus which, for a period of forty-eight hours, confined Crooks, Gregory, Myler and others to their beds. With constant visits to the hospital for X-rays by Goodway (elbow injury), and with visits by the doctor to the flu victims, it was not surprising that the morale of the party dropped.

Nor were matters helped by the fact that this particular Monday was the coldest July day Sydney had experienced for eighty-eight years. By Wednesday, however, as the 'flu victims recovered and most of the injuries cleared, there was an air of optimism again along the corridors of the Sheraton-Wentworth hotel, even though the coach was unable to decide on his team. Frank Myler may have said that he was 'undecided on his forward formation' and that 'the final choice of front row will be Brian Noble's', but in truth he had few options. Mick Adams was the only player left to fill the loose-forward position, as Mick Worrall, who had to have a minor cartilage operation, joined the injury list with Pinner and Flanagan. As Crooks and Rayne were unavailable to prop, Hobbs and Case were the obvious choices in that position. Brian Case especially deserved his chance and, determined that nothing would stop him playing, was eager to grasp it. He hastily moved out of the room he had been sharing with 'flu victim Lee Crooks to find accommodation elsewhere.

Despite the martial sound and colourful array of the Marching Koalas, one of Sydney's most famous bands, and the boos which greeted Mick Adams and David Hobbs as they appeared on the giant video screen which now adorns the 'hill', the pre-match atmosphere was as grey and overcast as the sky. Indeed, the match itself was sluggish and dull. There were a few golden moments for British fans when victory was sensed – but, alas, not achieved.

Neither side had been happy with referee Ray Shrimpton's performances in the previous two Tests, and both had requested a change. And Sydney's daily papers, anticipating that a few personal feuds might be carried over from those final ten minutes at Lang Park, generally welcomed the appointment of another New Zealander, Tony Drake, as referee. But his task on the field was made easier by the management of both camps, who promised a crackdown on foul play. All this conspired to produce a very clean game, which never needed either physiotherapist on the pitch.

Perhaps because the destination of the Ashes Trophy had already been

21. With the ball secure under his arm and the sniff of a try in his nostrils, the Australian second-row forward Wayne Pearce makes yet another awesome charge at the heart of the Lions' defence in the third Test at Sydney. Pearce was deservedly voted man-of-the-series.

decided, there was, after the first half, an inevitability about the outcome of the game which hushed the 18,756 spectators. But for the first thirty-three minutes of the match, the noise made by the British contingent in the crowd more than compensated for the silence later.

Despite two shocking misses at goal in the fifth and sixth minutes by

Meninga, Australia led by a single penalty goal when he atoned for his previous failures in front of the posts by kicking a penalty from 5 yards out, following an offside at a drop-out. Australia attacked incessantly for the first twenty minutes, but the tackling of Adams, Noble and Goodway meant that they started to lose much of their midfield composure. Second-row and man-of-the-match Wayne Pearce was dumped unceremoniously on the floor by Noble, and wing Eric Grothe crashed to the ground in a low covering tackle by Keith Mumby. The Australian captain, Wally Lewis, soon realized that there were few gaps in the British defence, so turned to kicking to try to open up the game. Yet the long raking punts to Hanley and Drummond and high 'bombs' on to Burke at full-back were all safely held. Stalemate ensued. For the first time in the series Britain, with tigerish tackling, drove Australia back 35 yards when in possession of the ball. And yet so strong was the Australian defence that until the twenty-third minute the Lions had not crossed the half-way line. Price, Pearce and Dowling in the pack had moved up so quickly to tackle that Britain's attack moved sideways, and players lost the ball on the second or third tackles with great regularity. Then came the moment for which the British fans had been waiting.

Tony Myler made the first clean break of the match, weaving his way past three players before being stopped on the half-way line. Hanley, forsaking his wing spot, took up the acting half-back position and, showing considerable strength, brushed off the tackles of Lewis and Niebling as he raced upfield. Once in the clear, he headed for the posts and for 25 yards managed to hold off both Grothe and Boustead, Australia's covering wings, to touch down beneath the posts. Burke converted, and with the score at 6–2 to the Lions, hopes began to rise. As in the previous two encounters with Schofield's tries, Britain had shown that for pace and flair their backs were the equal of the Kangaroos in attack. That flair was exhibited ten minutes later when Neil Holding dropped the cheekiest of goals to increase the lead. For that one golden moment, as the British players raced back upfield for the kick-off, hearts raced in anticipation of an unexpected win.

Australia were ill at ease, despite a further Meninga penalty goal, awarded for one of many offside decisions given against the Lions by Mr Drake. Steve Mortimer, who had been brought into the team as replacement for the injured Murray, resorted to kicking – a high 'bomb' and then a chip kick over the defence – but Britain held firm. Union Jacks were waving on the 'hill'; banners were unfurled in the grandstands proclaiming 'The Poms are the Greatest'. The end of a long line of Test defeats was in sight. But in the history of Test rugby between Australia and Britain there have been players like Reg Gasnier, Wally Lewis, Keith Holman, Alec Murphy, Roger Millward and Alan Prescott who in an inspired moment have turned the result of a game. The

93

15-stone, bearded Parramatta wing, Eric Grothe, can now be added to that list of legendary names.

On the Sunday before the Test Grothe had given warning of his form by equalling his club's match scoring record with four tries. Yet few expected him to score a minute before half-time when hooker Greg Conescu lobbed the ball to Meninga with Britain's cover streaming across the field. Meninga passed the ball to Grothe, only 10 yards from the British try-line but barely a yard from the touchline, with Schofield and the strong-tackling Burke bearing down on him. Of present-day wingers I am sure only Grothe could have scored that try. A change of pace and a swing of the hips was enough to put Schofield off-balance and easily knocked aside. Within two yards he was faced with Burke, usually a fiercesome sight himself at 14 stone, and yet Grothe charged at the full-back, ducked low in order to ride the tackle, and miraculously avoided stepping into touch. His try, shown at least six times from every conceivable angle on the giant screen, brought cries of rapture from the Australian fans. The killer blow had been struck; Australia went in at half-time to an 8–7 lead and the Test, as a contest, was over.

Brian Noble, as well as taking two scrums against the head, had led his team well, and his example in defence, and in attack from the acting half-back position, was an inspiration to others. Hobbs and Case at prop gave him good support in the second half, and Goodway and Burton were willing to drive the ball at every opportunity. But all their effort and energy were unable to break the stranglehold which the Australian tackling put on them. Indeed, for fully twenty minutes in the second half, the Lions were penned in their own 25-yard area and, lacking the size and pace in the forwards to make a break, were forced to play out the full complement of six tackles on two occasions without making 10 yards of ground. Australia, on the other hand, created chances for tries through strong forward drives from Dowling and Pearce and, when the ball was transferred to Boustead or Miles, it took good covering by Myler and Mumby to relieve the danger.

With Britain unable to throw off the continuous pressure, it was obvious that Australia would score again, as they did when Conescu slipped the tackles of Myler and Burke when running from the acting half-back position. Their second try, only seven minutes from the end, came from more imaginative play, a movement covering 40 yards and involving Mortimer, Jack, Pearce and Boustead interpassing at speed, before Jack scurried for the posts. Meninga's two conversions edged Australia to 20 points, a winning margin of only 13 points but enough to create another 3–0 triumph and the tenth consecutive Test win against Great Britain.

In the subdued after-match atmosphere the players maintained the tradition of swapping jerseys as they left the pitch, while the Australian vice-captain,

22. Sadly, the third Test in Sydney was the last of Ray Price's international career. The veteran Australian loose forward had given stalwart service to his country and it was fitting that skipper Wally Lewis should bear him triumphantly from the pitch as Australia completed another whitewash of Great Britain.

Ray Price, was borne aloft on the shoulders of a colleague as a tribute to his farewell Test match. Wayne Pearce, Australia's man-of-the-series, and Britain's Andy Goodway, named by the visiting press as Britain's most effective player, exchanged pleasantries as they left the Cricket Ground, each heading for different dressing-rooms, the Australians' full of noise, laughter and frothing beer cans, the British silent but also full of frothing beer cans. To the victors only the taste is different.

In this third Test the Australians had based their success on an impregnable defence, with a back line a stone and a half per man heavier than Britain's. Moreover, in Wayne Pearce and Eric Grothe they had two players who could stamp their class on a game and affect the outcome of the Ashes. Their coach, Frank Stanton, was now able to relax in the knowledge that he had become the most successful international coach Rugby League has produced in winning four Ashes series both at home and abroad. For Britain's coach, Frank Myler, the search for that elusive Test win still remained despite the meticulous preparation. For him there was no rest, only more hard work for the equally daunting task of the encounters across the Tasman Sea in New Zealand.

Australia: Jack (Balmain, Sydney); Boustead (Manly, Sydney), Miles (Wynnum-Manly, Brisbane), Meninga (Souths, Brisbane), Grothe (Parramatta, Sydney); Lewis (Wynnum-Manly, Brisbane) captain, Mortimer (Canterbury-Bankstown, Sydney); Niebling (Redcliffe, Brisbane), Conescu (Gladstone, Brisbane), Dowling (Wynnum-Manly, Brisbane), Fullerton-Smith (Redcliffe, Brisbane), Pearce (Balmain, Sydney), Price (Parramatta, Sydney)

Substitutes: Brown (Manly, Sydney) for Fullerton-Smith after 62 minutes, Kenny (Parramatta, Sydney) for Miles after 68 minutes

Scorers: tries – Grothe, Conescu, Jack; goals – Meninga (4)

Great Britain: Burke (Widnes); Drummond (Leigh), Schofield (Hull), Mumby (Bradford Northern), Hanley (Bradford Northern); Myler (Widnes), Holding (St Helens); Hobbs (Featherstone Rovers), Noble (Bradford Northern) captain, Case (Wigan), Burton (Hull KR), Goodway (Oldham), Adams (Widnes)

Substitutes: Smith (Hull KR), Rayne (Leeds) not used

Scorers: try – Hanley; goal – Burke; drop goal – Holding

Referee: T. Drake (New Zealand)

Attendance: 18,756

6

THE LIONS IN NEW ZEALAND
AND PAPUA NEW GUINEA

Though Britain's dominance was almost total in the first sixty-two years of Tests against New Zealand – Britain winning 12–2 in all series of two matches or more – no one has doubted the quality of individual Kiwi players. Before 1970 New Zealand's inferiority as a Test team was largely due to lack of depth in the game there, dominated as New Zealand is by Rugby Union, and to the fact that all the clubs are amateur. Individual players have been the equal of any in the world and many, as we have seen from those playing for British clubs, were and are superior. Take, for example, players like Lou Brown, the Maori three-quarter who played for Wigan in the 1920s, scoring 224 tries in his career, and Brian Nordgren (Wigan) and Peter Henderson (Huddersfield), two flying wings of the 1940s and 1950s, who followed the great tradition of Kiwi wingers, begun in the early pioneer days by the sprinter George Smith. Another was Cec Mountford, the brilliant little stand-off who played for Wigan and Warrington and graced the British game between 1947 and 1974, not only as a player but as a highly successful manager of Warrington and Blackpool. Nor will Lance Todd ever be forgotten now that his name is commemorated by the trophy presented to the man-of-the-match every year in the Challenge Cup final at Wembley. Such an honour was given in recognition of his services to the game as a player with Wigan, as manager of the famous Salford team of the 1930s, and as a popular BBC radio broadcaster. Indeed, the contribution of New Zealanders to the strength and popularity of British Rugby League has been immense. Yet, despite the quality of their players, it is only since 1970 that New Zealand have begun to achieve success with their national team.

The closeness of the 1980 Test series against Great Britain, with the Kiwis coached by Cec Mountford, was to bring the New Zealand game to the front of world rugby. Sadly for Britain, in the light of her experiences in 1982 against Australia, the British game was only stirred not shaken.

The squad of twenty-six players which arrived in 1980 was the first New Zealand party to visit Britain since the Test series in 1971, when the Kiwis had recorded an astonishing 2–1 victory. After an opening canter against Blackpool Borough, almost 16,000 fans saw them score nine tries to romp home over Hull at Boothferry Park. A score of 33–10, against one of the most feared clubs in Britain, should have alarmed the British team. The message, unfortunately, did not sink in. However, New Zealand recognized that they had a goalkicking problem – there were only three successful attempts at goal in the Hull match – and that this was likely to diminish their overall playing record during the tour and perhaps be one of the determining factors in the Test series. But founded on solid defence, first formulated by Cec Mountford during his coaching days with Warrington, the team never conceded more than 15 points in any match on the fourteen-game tour. The New Zealand Test side, captained by the loose forward Mark Graham, introduced exciting runners to the British public, many of whom would be playing for British teams twelve months after the tour.

New Zealand were thought to be unlucky only to draw 14–14 at Wigan in the first Test. Their forwards, especially Mark Broadhurst, Graeme West and Mark Graham, were exceptionally mobile in their support play, while the half-back partnership of Fred Ah Kuoi and Gordon Smith dominated the British pairing of Steve Hartley (Hull KR) and Kevin Dick (Leeds). Indeed, the Kiwi pair scored 11 of the points with Smith kicking four goals and Ah Kuoi going over for a try. Ah Kuoi was also given the man-of-the-match award for his shrewd play. The Great Britain manager, Colin Hutton, readily acknowledged: 'Ah Kuoi is setting us some problems, standing deep and dictating play, making him very difficult to neutralize.' It was not only Ah Kuoi who was to prove 'difficult to neutralize', for at Odsal Stadium, Bradford, in November the New Zealand side won a Test for the first time on that ground by 12–8, to go one-up in the series.

Despite an opening goal from the captain, George Fairbairn, in the fourth minute, New Zealand never appeared threatened as they took a half-time lead of 9–6, thanks to three goals from scrum-half Gordon Smith and a try from the adventurous full-back Michael O'Donnell who, in a particularly well worked move, outpaced both Camilleri and Fairbairn to score at the corner. Four goals from Fairbairn closed the gap to 9–8 in New Zealand's favour, but such was the defensive ability of the side that Britain rarely looked like scoring a try. The back-row trio of West, Coll and Graham, until his substitution by Baxendale in the second half, maintained a vice-like grip on any would-be British attackers, and it came as no surprise when the only try of the second half went to New Zealand's winger, Dane O'Hara, in the sixty-seventh minute to seal victory.

That the series was eventually drawn was due to Britain making large-scale changes in their team, especially in the pack, where they recalled three old campaigners in Skerrett (Hull), Adams (Widnes) and Norton (Hull). It was their experience which was able to fashion a workmanlike win, 10–2, in the third Test at Headingley, Leeds, though once again the exciting play stemmed from the Kiwis. They had come very close to inflicting another Test series defeat on Britain, and once again that vital factor, pride, had been uppermost in many of the players' minds. They had wanted to show the British crowds not only that their skills were second to none but also the extent to which the League game in New Zealand had advanced. Their captain, Mark Graham, summed up his team's feelings when he spoke to John Huxley of the *Sunday Mirror*: 'We are on tour at the same time as the Rugby Union All Blacks and, quite naturally, we want the rugby public back home to see that we are doing as well as, if not better than, they are. To have done well in Britain will do our game a great deal of good and we are anxious to make sure of that progress.'

The progress made by New Zealand players during the past few years was such that, of that tour party, eleven returned to play for British League clubs. Hull, in particular, owe much of their success in recent seasons to Gary Kemble, James Leuluai, Fred Ah Kuoi and Dane O'Hara, while Mark Broadhurst, Gary Prohm and Gordon Smith of Hull Kingston Rovers, Graeme West and Howard Tamati of Wigan, Kevin Tamati of Widnes and Shane Varley of Workington and Leigh have done much to improve the fortunes of their adopted clubs.

At the start of the 1980 tour the manager and coach, Cec Moutford, illustrated the vitality of Rugby League in New Zealand when he said: 'Playing-wise it is in tremendous health. There are sixteen leagues right from the top of North Island to the bottom of South Island. We are blessed with a thriving schools game, and eight universities are currently playing Rugby League.' Indeed, the coaching schemes which he himself has helped to introduce have been largely responsible for producing the present crop of fine players. After the struggles of the early days when Rugby League goal-posts used to be chopped down and pitches ploughed up, the present climate for Rugby League in New Zealand is very favourable. Certainly it is now unlikely that, as in the early 1950s, schoolboys in Otago will be hauled on stage before a full school assembly for daring to play Rugby League.

The administration of the game in New Zealand has been streamlined with the employment of a full-time executive director and a national coach. More coverage is given to the game by the media, especially by television, while the new national club championship has provided a sound basis for internal competition. One of the biggest single factors in the growth of the code has been the emergence of sponsorship, particularly from Autex Industries in 1979, a company whose directors have a strong north of England association. Their support of Rugby League provided the financial base for the successful tour of

23.   Leaving behind the hard pitches of Australia, the battle-weary Lions moved on to New Zealand and altogether different playing conditions. In the mud and rain of Carlaw Park, Auckland, during the first Test on 14 July, Great Britain gave one of their most disappointing performances. Although a desperate tackle by Mick Burke halted prop forward Dane Sorenson just short of the line on this occasion, the Kiwis scored two tries in their 12–0 victory.

Britain and France in 1980 and for the drawn series with the Australians in 1983. Because of that support the game has now acquired important sponsorship, with firms like KB, Sony, Teleras and Wrangler/Tusk contributing large sums to the game. Perhaps the most widely publicized sponsorship, through television and radio, comes from a firm of butchers called 'The Mad Butcher', whose owner has done as much as anyone to bring the excitement of Rugby League to the public's attention.

The outward signs of good health were evident in New Zealand agreeing to undertake two major overseas tours to Britain in October and November 1983 – by the New Zealand Universities and by the Maoris. The universities' tour was a sign of the growth of the game at college level and was most welcome in Britain where a similar development is now making rapid strides. Commenting at the time on the Maoris' tour, which took place at the request of the British Amateur Rugby League Association, Tom Newton, chairman of the Maori Board of Control, remarked, '1983 is the year that the Maori Board of Control will be able to reflect on as their best year of progress and contribution to the Rugby League game.'

Indeed, the Maori influence on Rugby League has developed remarkably since the two Asher brothers, Opai and Ernie, organized the first 'All Native New Zealand Rugby League' side to tour Australia in 1908. The Maoris, who set up their Board of Control in 1934 at Huntly to help expand the game, could hardly have envisaged the influence their players now have on Rugby League outside New Zealand: players such as Nick Wright (Oldham), Dean Bell (Leeds) and Pat Poasa (Warrington) stayed behind in Britain after the 1983 tour to further increase New Zealand's close connections with British Rugby League.

However, alongside progress and success have come problems. It has been suggested that a national club competition should be started in New Zealand on a league basis, with the top twelve clubs in the country taking part in a home and away series. This would not only provide the best players with regular competition but would also create a platform for the promotion of the game on a national basis. Their star players might then be less inclined to seek their fortune overseas. It is a sad fact that though the New Zealand authorities receive a cash sum every time one of their players joins a foreign club, the departure of so many leading players cannot be to the ultimate good of the home game. Rugby League in New Zealand has always been amateur, but is currently producing players of world class. This is a major problem and one which Ron McGregor, chairman of the New Zealand R.L. council, says must be solved if the future of domestic Rugby League is to be secured, 'Whereas in earlier days most of our internationals were content to remain in New Zealand, and play as amateurs, the situation is now changed and we have a growing number of Rugby League players who see professional Rugby League as part of their future. Until we can establish a professional competition in New Zealand, we will continue to lose them to other countries. The problem must be solved if we are to strengthen and develop the code in New Zealand. Obviously it must be on a limited scale to start with and in a different format from the present, but it is the most important challenge of the future.'

However, the biggest threat to the future of Rugby League may come from outside, in the shape of the New Zealand Rugby Union bending to pressure from its own players for some relaxation of the more draconian laws which relate to their amateur status. Any trend towards semi- or full professionalism in the Union game would have devastating effects on recruitment for the amateur League game, an ironic twist to the original cause of the split between the two codes!

The 1984 Lions landed at Auckland immediately after the Sydney Test to start the New Zealand leg of their tour. Somewhat battle weary, they were welcomed by the sight of green grass and soft earth, and the thought of playing rugby in conditions they were far more familiar with. The atmosphere in New Zealand was more relaxed, the people by nature quieter than Australians, but their attitude towards rugby is no less fervent. They were still rejoicing at their newly gained status of world champions after the defeat of Australia at Brisbane the previous season. And they were not averse to a little bit of psychological warfare. The words of New Zealand's coach, Graham Lowe, in a radio broadcast calling New Zealanders 'to give them (the Lions) a taste of Kiwi' could not have encouraged the British players who had already been defeated in three Tests. Nor could the prophecy made by the *New Zealand Times* correspondent, Bernie Wood, that 'New Zealand will win all three Tests in an unprecedented whitewash' have filled the players with confidence as they settled down to a restful evening in their hotel overlooking the bay. Whatever the merits of such a propaganda exercise, the squad, now lacking the services of Rod McKenzie who had had to return to England to continue his duties at Carnegie College, was hard at training the next day for the first match at Whangarei.

Frank Myler was under no illusions about the difficulty of the task, rightly pointing out, 'The days of easy tours to New Zealand are over.' His work for the match against Northern Districts and for the first Test concentrated on movement around the play-the-balls and plays to ensure the quick movement of the ball out wide to the wings. Throughout Australia, Myler's biggest disappointment had been that 'the team has often been pedestrian in making play from the play-the-balls and too often, when under pressure, has resorted to one-man plunges.' A further attempt was made to sort out this aspect of the game, while skipper Brian Noble helped with the physical exercise work, and most energetically too. Having asked me to time the players, I can vouch for the harshness of his passing routines. Lydon, Drummond, Hanley and Goodway even urged me to knock a few seconds off my timing, but I did not yield to their pleas.

102

Few people gave the Northern Districts much hope of success in the Lions' first match at Jubilee Park, Whangarei. Most of the spectators were simply happy to know that their side of enthusiastic amateurs had done their best. Indeed, after sixty minutes play they had contained a somewhat lethargic touring side to a 16–8 lead, and had made the visitors struggle for every try. Only Kevin Beardmore, who won a camera for being man-of-the-match, and prop David Hobbs played to their full potential, though the Widnes pair, Andy Gregory and Mick Adams, worked hard in midfield to create a try for each other as well as having a part to play in others from Basnett, Proctor, Clark, Beardmore, Joyner and Smith.

The casual attitude throughout the day was prompted by the carnival atmosphere surrounding the game, which had followed a leisurely trip from Auckland round sandy bays, washed by the shimmering blue sea of the Pacific, dense forests, lakes and ravines. Jubilee Park itself provided the most unlikely setting for a major rugby match. The excellent pitch, surrounded for the most part by eager Maori faces, was set alongside a white wooden hut, inside which hung the prized possession of a faded sepia-brown photograph recording the visit of the 1936 Great Britain team to the same ground. It was obvious that the ground had not changed from that day! Nor, I imagined, had the people. Here were the real grass roots of New Zealand Rugby League, with unlimited hospitality from the warm-hearted officials and the large contingent of Maoris who entertained the party. From the half-time rugby game between two teams of 6-year-old boys and girls, playing in bare feet, to the after-match Hangi, the traditional Maori feast cooked on hot stones covered by earth, it was a fascinating experience for everyone, not least the players who mingled freely, signing countless autographs for the youngsters. It was also fascinating for the onlookers who witnessed a BBC correspondent scale a barbed-wire fence to ring his match report through to Britain on a public telephone in the ladies' toilet of a nearby caravan site, there being no suitable telephone available in the white hut.

For Test centre Keith Mumby, concussed early in the second half of the match, the day had ended on a sore note, but Ron Barritt was not too concerned. When he asked Mumby what day it was, as a means of checking the after-effects of his heavy knock, Keith replied correctly, 'Tuesday.' His next reply, when asked where the team was playing, eased Ron's worries: 'I know where we are but I can't pronounce it.' He was declared fit! (**Final score: Northern Districts 8   Great Britain 42.**)

First Test
Auckland, 14 July
New Zealand 12   Great Britain 0

The city of Auckland reserved its usual greeting for British touring teams when, beginning late on the Friday evening, the rains descended. By the time of the 2.30 p.m. kick-off for the Test match the following day there were seagulls landing on the pitch with great regularity, and the spectators, mostly clad in the brightest yellow oilskin parkas, huddled beneath the grandstands to avoid the torrential downpour. They were in good spirits, however, as their full-throated rendering of the national anthem indicated.

Injury problems had followed the British party to New Zealand and forwards Pinner, Rayne, Worrall and Flanagan were all unavailable for this match. Centres Smith and Joyner were therefore selected as substitutes because they had experience of playing at loose forward. But worse was to befall the team, and as they stood on the pitch, heads bowed, it was as if they were bemoaning the dramatic last-minute withdrawal of Tony Myler. Myler's luck had failed again when he was forced to cry off from the side at noon with food poisoning – a withdrawal which was to take away the Lions' real strength in midfield and the one midfield back able to make play for others. Mike Smith, the experienced Test centre, was brought in to partner Neil Holding at half-back but it was a combination that was found wanting as the game progressed.

The first ten minutes of the match offered opportunities which could have sealed the game for the Lions. Twice they broke clean through the Kiwi ranks, once when Holding sped away, but chip-kicked too soon over the full-back Kemble's head, and was beaten in the race for the ball. And within minutes Mick Adams sold an outrageous dummy and raced upfield where Goodway was on hand to collect the inside pass. Only alert covering by the wing, Dean Bell, who felled Goodway with what looked suspiciously like a high tackle, saved the situation for New Zealand. With the exception of one run, late in the second half by Hanley, the Lions never again threatened to score and were gripped tight by New Zealand for the next seventy minutes. New Zealand's tactics in those first ten minutes told how they would succeed, using tactical kicking, allied to a strong defence.

Twice the burly full-back Mick Burke was forced to field high kicks from his opposite number Kemble; and throughout the match Varley, Filipaina and especially Kemble were to plague Hanley on Britain's left wing by making him turn and retrieve the ball, after long raking punts to the corner. The Kiwi wing,

24.   Ellery Hanley, as he had done in Australia, produced one of the few exciting moments for Great Britain in the first Test against New Zealand at Auckland. After a thrilling sixty-yard dash, he just failed to outpace full-back Gary Kemble, New Zealand's last line of defence.

Bell, followed up the kicks at great speed and was able to contain Hanley or Burke close to the British try-line with some tigerish tackling. A combination of strong running from Kurt Sorenson and, later, from the 15-stone stand-off Olsen Filipaina, enabled the speedy centres Leuluai and Ah Kuoi to take passes and score in the nineteenth and thirty-seventh minutes. Filipaina's conversions took the score to 12–0 in New Zealand's favour and, in effect, the game was over.

With pools of water now forming on the pitch and the rain unrelenting in its intensity, the Lions returned for the second half clad in a new set of jerseys, but their play during the next forty minutes was the dullest and most tactically inept of the whole tour. As in the second half of the third Test in Australia, the British pattern of play was so stereotyped that for thirty minutes they did not even cross the half-way line. The tackling of Kevin Tamati and the Sorenson brothers was first-class, but it was not difficult to cope with Britain's lack of imagination and variety at the play-the-balls. The tactics consisted of the acting half-back, usually Brian Noble, taking the ball upfield himself, or Mick Adams passing the ball to a charging forward. This was drearily monotonous play! Britain's efforts to break free from the Kiwi stranglehold consisted of little chip kicks in the 25-yard area, kicks which, in contrast to those of New Zealand, only put pressure on themselves. There was a distinct lack of ideas from the loose-forward and half-backs triangle in midfield, while, in contrast, Varley at scrum-half and the loose forward McGahan for New Zealand ranged far and wide distributing the ball to colleagues in support. The play of the Kiwi forwards in midfield and the backing-up of centres Leuluai and Ah Kuoi were an object lesson to our leaden-footed players.

Before the match, Graham Lowe, the Kiwi coach, had said in praise of the Lions, 'Great Britain will be harder to beat than Australia, for Australia have a pattern of play that can be read. Great Britain do not have a game plan but have brilliant individuals with natural ability.' As the team's bus drove away from Carlaw Park, its radio sarcastically playing 'Raindrops Keep Falling on my Head', I am sure that many were wondering whether Graham Lowe, too, was unwittingly being sarcastic when he referred to Great Britain's lack of a 'game plan'. Frank Myler must have wondered whether his players did in fact realize that they had possessed one.

New Zealand: Kemble (Auckland & Hull); O'Hara (Auckland & Hull), Leuluai (Auckland & Hull), Ah Kuoi (Auckland & Hull) captain, Bell (Auckland & Leeds); Filipaina (Balmain, Sydney), Varley (Auckland & Leigh); Kevin Tamati (Wellington & Widnes), Howie Tamati (Taranaki & Wigan), Dane Sorenson (Eastern Suburbs, Sydney), Kurt Sorenson (Eastern Suburbs, Sydney), Wright (Auckland), McGahan (Auckland)

Substitutes: Friend (Auckland) for Filipaina after 78 minutes, Cowan (Auckland) not used

Scorers: tries – Leuluai, Ah Kuoi; goals – Filipaina (2)

Great Britain: Burke (Widnes); Drummond (Leigh), Mumby (Bradford Northern), Schofield (Hull), Hanley (Bradford Northern); Smith (Hull KR), Holding (St Helens); Hobbs (Featherstone Rovers), Noble (Bradford Northern) captain, Case (Wigan), Goodway (Oldham), Burton (Hull KR), Adams (Widnes)

Substitutes: Gregory (Widnes), Joyner (Castleford) not used

Referee: K. Roberts (Australia)

Attendance: 8,500

Any plans for the second Test at Christchurch, only eight days away, had to be shelved until the following Thursday after the Lions had negotiated two further hurdles against the Maoris at Huntly and Central Districts at Wellington.

It was expected that the match against the Maoris, on the Sunday following the first Test, would be a hard one and that a hostile welcome would await the players on the field. It was not to be, however, and Britain had little trouble in coasting to victory. From the announcer at the game who boomed out with great regularity, 'Give them a big welcome', to the elders who prepared a lavish spread of food at the after-match reception, the Maori hospitality was impressive. But Joe Lydon did not think so for, receiving a blow to the back of the head in the twentieth minute of the match, he staggered around concussed until he was replaced by Hanley. Britain had too much pace for the Maoris and Foy's try after only twenty-five minutes showed how Hanley, Drummond and Foy himself were able to prise open the gaps in defence when necessary. Beardmore's try and then Flanagan's were due to good work by Flanagan himself who revelled in the fact that he was at last free from the troublesome ankle injury which had restricted him to only three games on the tour. Gregory, as well as helping himself to a drop goal, appeared to be more at home in the heavier conditions of New Zealand and formed an effective partnership at half-back with Joyner, the skipper for the day. (**Final score: Maoris 8 Great Britain 19.**)

It was forecast that Central Districts would present little serious opposition to the Lions three days later, and indeed the problems encountered at the Hutt recreation ground, Wellington, were few compared with the troubles in the forty-eight hours prior to the match. The injuries to Worrall and Pinner had still not cleared, and the forward position worsened with the news that a nose broken in the Maori game would keep Proctor out for a couple of weeks. Moreover, the prospect of Crooks playing again on tour had decreased after his failure yet again to stay the full eighty minutes. He was still restricted by his painful shoulder tendons. Worse was to come! Garry Schofield, after a precautionary visit to hospital, following some pain in his leg while training, arrived back at the hotel supporting the largest of plaster casts round his foot. Apparently a stress fracture of his shin had been discovered, which was to rule him out of all further games on tour. It was a bitter blow to Britain's Test hopes. Frank Myler, peering through the hotel reception windows at the rain cascading down on Auckland, wryly observed, 'It never rains but it pours.'

Then both Myler and Ron Barritt suffered food poisoning in the two days prior to the Central Districts game. Unable to attend training on the Tuesday, they had to be told by the manager, Dick Gemmell, that Ray Ashton's disc trouble had not responded to treatment and that he had broken down during the training session. He, too, would not play again on tour. However, in the Central Districts match there was an excellent display from Andy Gregory who, as well as grabbing a couple of tries for himself, had a hand in the other five scored by Noble (2), Clark, Donlan, and Smith. With five goals, from Burke (4) and Lydon, the Lions ended easy winners. With no more injuries to report, Myler and Barritt could shake off their ailments with a good night's sleep. (**Final score: Central Districts 6   Great Britain 38.**)

**Second Test
Christchurch, 22 July
New Zealand 28   Great Britain 12**

Rest was the order of the day for the tourists as Dick Gemmell placed a curfew on his players prior to the second Test. In fact, the players were only too ready to relax at night at their headquarters on the outskirts of Christchurch, all well aware of how much they needed a Test victory.

A stomach disorder suffered by prop Brian Case, and slight glandular trouble with Mick Burke, delayed selection until the Friday evening when both were declared fit. There had been few doubts about Burke's eventual availability; his main concern was that the doctor had advised him to stop eating for a couple of days – disastrous news to a 14-stone full-back with a more than healthy appetite! There was good news, too, for his Widnes colleagues, Gregory and Lydon, whose form in Australia had not reached expectations. Gregory came into the side instead of Holding whose persistent knee and groin problems made him unavailable for selection. In fairness, Gregory's fine performances in New Zealand would have won him the place on merit. With Hanley's move to centre, as cover for the injured Schofield, the logical successor on the wing was Lydon, as Myler realized the need for attacking potential rather than the solid defensive qualities that would have come first in Australia. Britain's back division now had players who could seize any opportunity, and turn a half chance into a try. They would not be subjected to the constant battering, as with the huge Australian back division, but would be faced with the more subtle skills of the fleet-footed Kiwis. New Zealand, confident of success, retained the same side. The only other change was the appointment of a new referee in

25. New Zealand were able to turn the screw in the second Test at Christchurch on 22 July. The Kiwi centre James Leuluai shows his speed as he breaks between full-back Mick Burke (left) and the despairing dive of Mick Adams to score New Zealand's first try.

Barry Barnes of Sydney, the fourth referee to make his international debut on the tour. Though an experienced referee of nineteen years' standing, he was a strange choice in view of the excellent control that Kevin Roberts had shown in the first Test.

Though the weather was again hostile with rain clouds rolling in over the nearby hills, the tourists were greeted with friendly applause from the few spectators who braved the elements. Nevertheless, the conditions did not prevent the Kiwis from giving a masterly display of their skills as they clinched the series.

Their triumph was based initially on the dominance of their pack which swept aside ineffective tackling and opened up huge gaps on which the back division capitalized. Once again, the two Sorenson brothers and Kevin Tamati bore the brunt of the midfield play, supporting each other cleverly as they tore at the heart of Britain's defence.

The back-row pair of Wright and McGahan hovered on the fringes and ran on to the ball from wide and deep positions, creating a variety of forward plays to which Britain had no answer. They frequently swept upfield for 30 or 40 yards before releasing the ball to the accompanying backs. Here again there was more planning and pattern to New Zealand's play, with scrum-half Varley always lurking behind a forward break and ready to open play out to his three-quarters, who proved far too skilful and fast for the opposing line. It was hoped that there would be some relief for the British back division after the physical assaults of the Australians, but in Christchurch, as in Auckland, the speed and skilful handling of the Kiwis' three-quarter line gave them little respite. Two of New Zealand's five tries, all scored by the three-quarter line, were a fitting tribute to the intentions of their coach, Graham Lowe, who had declared that he intended to play thirteen-man rugby, whatever the conditions.

A record played over the public address system at half-time implored New Zealand to 'Give 'em a taste of Kiwi', and they certainly did with two of their efforts in the second half. After barely five minutes, a break by Ah Kuoi in his own half threw the Lions' retreating defence into disarray, especially when McGahan was on hand in the right centre position to continue the movement. Brushing off some pathetic shoulder charges which passed for tackling, McGahan was able to combine with Filipaina and Leuluai in a bout of high-speed passing before the wing, Dean Bell, completed the movement to score.

A similar movement fifteen minutes later illustrated again New Zealand's ability to combine their forward breaks with intelligent distribution to their backs who were only too eager to accept the chances. Two powerful plunges from Dane and Kurt Sorenson took play over the half-way line where Kevin Tamati received the pass which enabled him to charge at two defenders outside Britain's 25-yard area. He skilfully drew the two defenders before placing the ball behind the back of his opponent and into the hands of centre Leuluai. Leuluai's pace and positional sense did the rest. He drew the cover on to himself before transferring the ball to his wing partner, O'Hara, who raced unopposed behind the posts. Here was crisp handling, strong running and good support play, in contrast to the predictable and unimaginative running of the Lions.

Despite Hanley and Myler scoring two well-worked tries from behind the scrums, displaying their understanding with full-back Burke, who linked up on both occasions, Britain did little to enliven the game. A 60-yard break by Goodway, continued by Hanley, who was unfortunate not to score when held over the try-line on his back, gave promise of better form in the opening fifteen minutes. It was not to be, as Britain found themselves penned in their own half for long stretches and with little idea of how to escape. As in the previous four Tests, when under pressure Britain had no player capable of assessing the situ-

26. One of the main reasons for the success of New Zealand in the third Test at Auckland on 28 July was the aggressive running of their forwards and the support play of the backs. The size and power of players like Olsen Filipaina, seen here drawing the Lions' back row out of position, enabled them only too often to smash through the ineffectual British tackling.

ation tactically and no one with the ability to ensure movement of the ball between forwards and backs. The result was that, despite all the hard graft in the forward drives by Hobbs, Noble and Case, the stereotyped play was easily countered by a strong New Zealand defence. Indeed, in the second half, Britain never crossed the half-way line by running or handling; only four deep kicks enabled them to gain a foothold in New Zealand's half. The crowd then waited patiently for New Zealand to regain possession.

The sharpness in the tackle, the eagerness to run with the ball and the desire to succeed, all shown by the Lions in Australia, had evaporated. When Frank Myler sympathetically replaced skipper Brian Noble with his understudy, Kevin Beardmore, sixteen minutes from the end, as a tribute to Beardmore's efforts on tour, it was the equivalent of raising a white flag. The match and the series, as a contest, were over and with five Tests played and five defeats, Britain's search for a Test victory was now taking on the proportions of the quest for the Holy Grail.

New Zealand: Kemble (Auckland & Hull); O'Hara (Auckland & Hull), Leuluai (Auckland & Hull), Ah Kuoi (Auckland & Hull) captain, Bell (Auckland & Leeds); Filipaina (Balmain, Sydney), Varley (Auckland & Leigh); Kevin Tamati (Wellington & Widnes), Howie Tamati (Taranaki & Wigan), Dane Sorenson (Eastern Suburbs, Sydney), Kurt Sorensen (Eastern Suburbs, Sydney), Wright (Auckland), McGahan (Auckland)

Substitutes: Friend (Auckland) for Varley after 73 minutes, Cowan (Auckland) for Howie Tamati after 73 minutes

Scorers: tries – O'Hara (2), Bell, Leuluai, Ah Kuoi; goals – Filipaina (4)

Great Britain: Burke (Widnes); Drummond (Leigh), Hanley (Bradford Northern), Mumby (Bradford Northern), Lydon (Widnes); Myler (Widnes), Gregory (Widnes); Hobbs (Featherstone Rovers), Noble (Bradford Northern) captain, Case (Wigan), Burton (Hull KR), Goodway (Oldham), Adams (Widnes)

Substitutes: Joyner (Castleford) for Burton after 45 minutes, Beardmore (Castleford) for Noble after 64 minutes

Scorers: tries – Myler, Hanley; goals – Burke (2)

Referee: B. Barnes (Australia)   Attendance: 3,800

Third Test
Auckland, 28 July
New Zealand 32   Great Britain 16

Anyone standing in the foyer of the Sheraton Hotel around midday on the Thursday following the second Test might have thought that all hope of a victory in the last match had disappeared completely. It was a tired and depressed party of players which trooped through the doors, following their flight from Christchurch that morning, delayed until the Thursday in order to accommodate the inconveniently-placed South Island fixture the previous evening. The comfortable win over South Island by 36–14 was significant for the sparkling form of Kevin Beardmore, who not only won the scrums but helped himself to a hat-trick of tries alongside those of John Basnett (2), Ellery Hanley and Keith Mumby. It was even more significant for the number of

27. The huge New Zealand second-row forward, Kurt Sorenson, brushes aside Andy Gregory's attempt at a smother-tackle as the Kiwis, in a late burst, romped to a 32–16 victory in the third Test at Auckland.

injuries incurred, injuries which, when added to those already sustained by the squad, meant that Frank Myler was able to select his final Test team from only seventeen players. Though Chris Burton (cut eye) and Mike O'Neill (sprung shoulder) were ruled out, the saddest injury was that to Kevin Beardmore, his damaged shoulder ligaments surely costing him a Test place.

Whatever the merits of playing a minor match so close to a Test, those players who were fit were at Auckland's Domain for yet another light training session within an hour of arrival. Options were extremely limited but, having decided not to risk Mick Worrall, who had not yet played in New Zealand, the coach selected Oldham's Terry Flanagan at loose forward and moved Mick

Adams into the second row. Flanagan's selection was reward for a player who had refused to bow to niggling injury problems in Australia. With his good form in recent matches, his inclusion was a sign that Britain hoped to play a more expansive game, with the loose forward distributing the ball to the backs.

New Zealand again had no problems, selecting the same side they had used throughout the series, and they trained in Auckland with considerable enthusiasm. There was little chance for any complacency in their camp with their coach insisting that, 'We are going for three wins in a row. The feat has never been achieved by a New Zealand team and we aim to be the first.'

The journey by coach from the team's hotel to the Addington Showgrounds, Christchurch, for the second Test had proved hilarious, even farcical, as the management struggled to play one of their 'motivational' cassettes over the address system. Unfortunately, they hadn't prepared the tape properly, and the team was treated to strains of Tchaikovsky instead of 'Eye of the Tiger' and 'Land of Hope and Glory'. The artificiality of the whole affair hit rock-bottom when the driver was instructed to go past the ground and to continue driving round while the managers continued to grapple with the tape.

Now when the team bus approached the wrought-iron gates of Carlaw Park for the third Test only pop music was blaring forth. There was to be no 'motivational' tape (of any sort) and no team songs – even the 'Ant Song' was forgotten. It was the final indication of the decline in the Lions' morale. I felt there was no way we could win the Test and confessed to Peter Wilson of the *Star* that we would lose by 30 points. Sadly, I was proved right.

For fifty-five minutes, however, Britain were on top for the first time in the series and kept a tight grip on New Zealand's free-flowing style of rugby, restricting them to one try in the twenty-eighth minute by O'Hara, the result of crisp handling and clever centre play from Leuluai. The Lions had learned how dangerous were the strong-running Kiwi forwards, closely supported by the pace of their backs, if they were allowed to keep possession near the British try-line. Hence, Burke and Hobbs kicked deep into the New Zealand half where, thanks to some strong tackling by Hobbs, Goodway and Adams, the Lions were able to maintain sufficient pressure to score. Tries from Mumby and Hanley, the latter a solo effort in which, following a break by Gregory, he beat O'Hara, Filipaina and Kemble on his way over the line, helped by Burke's four cleanly struck goals, gave the Lions a comfortable lead of 16–8.

But the euphoria soon vanished as coach Graham Lowe's substitution of Clayton Friend for Shane Varley in the fifty-second minute proved a master stroke. After taking two or three minutes to adjust to the speed of play, Friend brought much greater pace to the midfield, and short passes began to launch the huge stand-off, Olsen Filipaina, at the heart of the British defence. Filipaina was too strong for Tony Myler and the rest of the backs. He burst

28.   In the third Test against New Zealand, Britain spent much of the time in their own half. Only long punts down field and occasional determined runs such as this from prop forward Brian Case, seen here evading the challenge of Hugh McGahan, temporarily cleared the pressure on the Lions' try-line.

through on numerous occasions and, with Britain unable to put him to the floor in the tackle, he set up two tries for Leuluai. In contrast, the tiny Clayton Friend showed his pace and guile to weave past bigger but slower opponents also to score two tries. Four tries in twenty-five minutes, plus four conversions from Filipaina, and New Zealand had registered their biggest ever score in a Test match against Great Britain. They had also taken the series 3–0, another first in the history of Test struggles between the two nations.

The traditional Haka dance performed by the Kiwis at the end of the match showed their delight. For the Lions, the dismissals to the sin-bin of Gregory and Goodway in the last twenty minutes indicated the frustrations of a well-beaten and dispirited touring team. They had promised much but had failed to grasp the opportunities for success.

New Zealand: Kemble (Auckland & Hull); O'Hara (Auckland & Hull), Leuluai (Auckland & Hull), Ah Kuoi (Auckland & Hull) captain, Bell (Auckland & Leeds); Filipaina (Balmain, Sydney), Varley (Auckland & Leigh); Kevin Tamati (Wellington & Widnes), Howie Tamati (Taranaki & Wigan), Dane Sorenson (Eastern Suburbs, Sydney), Kurt Sorenson (Eastern Suburbs, Sydney), Wright (Auckland), McGahan (Auckland)

Substitutes: Friend (Auckland) for Varley after 52 minutes, Cowan (Auckland) for McGahan after 71 minutes

Scorers: tries – O'Hara, Leuluai (2), Friend (2); goals – Filipaina (6)

Great Britain: Burke (Widnes); Drummond (Leigh), Hanley (Bradford Northern), Mumby (Bradford Northern), Lydon (Widnes); Myler (Widnes), Gregory (Widnes); Hobbs (Featherstone Rovers), Noble (Bradford Northern) captain, Case (Wigan), Adams (Widnes), Goodway (Oldham), Flanagan (Oldham)

Substitutes: Joyner (Castleford) for Case after 58 minutes, Donlan (Leigh) for Burke after 71 minutes

Scorers: tries – Mumby, Hanley; goals – Burke (4)

Referee: K. Roberts (Australia)

Attendance: 7,500

The tour, in effect, was over. Brian Noble led his players dejectedly from the field, knowing that they had become the team with the worst Test record in the history of tours to Australia and New Zealand. Once off the field, they sought seclusion; and though they would have to re-emerge against Auckland, again under the glare of the Carlaw Park floodlights, in two days' time, the party was more than ready to fly home.

That final evening against Auckland saw the heaviest rainfall of the trip, as if the elements were registering their disapproval of events both on and off the field. They were right to do so for, despite sterling performances from Burke,

Gregory, Goodway and Rayne, the Lions' performance in their defeat that night was most disappointing. In contrast, the Auckland team displayed handling and support play of the highest quality with forwards Tamati, Wright and Ackland linking up at speed in imaginative movements with their centres, Bell and O'Regan. Though the result hinged on the final kick of the match, taken after the hooter had blown, Cedric Lovett's extra 2 points were deserved.

What was not deserved by the New Zealand and Auckland officials, and by the match sponsors at the farewell reception, was the failure of the manager or coach to attend and respond to the toasts of farewell. Thankfully, the impromptu speeches made by Brian Noble and the business manager, Roland Davis, did much to cement the friendly relations which had existed among the players of both sides throughout the tour. (**Final score: Auckland 18   Great Britain 16.**)

Though the rain in Auckland was followed by even worse weather in Papua New Guinea, the match at Mount Hagen provided a successful conclusion to the tour. The sight of over 7,000 people crowded into the tiny ground, with many thousands locked outside or perched in trees around the perimeter, was an indication of how important this fixture was to this emerging Rugby League country. The enthusiastic spectators inside the ground and those outside, who were told of the progress of the game by a lively announcer on the public address system, will remember the Lions' visit all their lives. And they certainly will never forget the fight back by their side when losing 4–22 at half-time. The Kumuls stunned Britain with a three-try onslaught in the first fifteen minutes of the second half. Though short of weight in the forwards, they had enough pace and flair to trouble the professionals for a short time, though the Lions had already won the game with four tries from Burke, Mumby, Drummond and Rayne in the first half.

Britain's victory was a consolation after their hard thirteen weeks' trek and the fans rose to them as they performed a lap of honour with their opponents. The wild enthusiasm of the spectators, the game itself, the hair-raising flight in bad weather from Madang to Mount Hagen, will all be remembered by the British players and officials. A British Lions' tour is about results and memories. Despite the bad results at Test level in Australia and New Zealand, Terry Flanagan, when commenting on the match against Papua New Guinea, summed up the tour for each of us: 'It was an experience not to be missed.'

7

THOUGHTS ON THE TOUR

Reflecting on the six lost Test matches, it is easy to conclude that the tour was a total failure. However, though there were certainly inadequacies and weaknesses in the touring party, there were successes, too, however slight, both on and off the field.

In Australia, following the 1982 débâcle, the Lions showed that they were once again a competitive force in world rugby. The three Test matches were absorbing contests, with Australia gaining the upper hand only in the closing quarters of each game. In fact, in the second and third Tests, there were times when Australia were in trouble, but unfortunately Britain were still not good enough to seize the initiative. Contrast this with the Tests of 1982 when Britain never looked like winning. Even statisticians would point to a narrowing of the gap in the quality of play. From scoring only one try and conceding 99 points against Australia in 1982, the Lions had improved sufficiently to score three tries and to restrict the Australians to 63 points in this series. By common consent, Britain's three tries were the pick of the matches and revealed running and handling skills of the highest order.

A significant improvement was in the team's fitness, where Britain invariably matched the Australians, and praise for this must go to Rod McKenzie for his work before and during the tour. His presence and ideas, when in Australia, brought organization to the training routines which were always varied, meticulously planned and interesting to the players. As a college lecturer, he knew the value of planning when dealing with young men who invariably need direction. And he was able to provide the kind of framework for training that is necessary to keep players' bodies and minds fresh and alert, if only as a counter to the debilitating effect of the monotony of a long tour. So long as Rod McKenzie assisted Frank Myler there was a sense of direction to the party's organization. His inability to travel to New Zealand was a disaster.

At 23 years of age and making his first tour 'down under', Brian Noble possibly lacked the tactical awareness that was necessary to be successful at the highest levels. As a captain, however, he lacked little else and, more than anyone, was responsible for creating the pride and ambition which were evident in the party. On the field and in training, he led by example. Off the field he performed many of the duties which should have been carried out by the manager. Though often apparently overburdened, he proved himself, along with his players, an excellent ambassador for the League game. His example and enthusiasm earned the respect of all and helped to create the correct attitude for the task of tackling the Australians at Test level.

The work performed by the coaching staff in strengthening Britain's defensive play was also excellent. In the weeks before and during the three Tests in Sydney and Brisbane, the party worked hard at defensive patterns with the use of tackling shields. The necessity to tackle hard and low was rammed into the players, with considerable success, which received due praise from an often hostile Australian press. But for the concentration on defence, the team would probably have struggled to win the praise of Ken Arthurson, the chairman of the Australian Rugby League, who, after the third Test, said, 'International Rugby is now alive and well. Among the tourists were some very capable and talented players whom I'm certain we will hear more of in years to come.' I would agree with that. And yet Britain lost the series by 0–3!

Defeated at Test level, but unbowed, there was reason to believe that things might come good in New Zealand. Sadly, injuries, illness and fatigue brought the tour to a disastrous end against skilful and highly motivated Kiwis. There was not even a glimpse of the form shown in the Tests in Australia. In the first two Tests and in the second half of the third Test, Britain were outclassed by superior tactics executed by more alert and skilful players, whose professionalism in many cases had been sharpened, ironically, in the British league. Only in the first half of the third Test did Britain provide a worthwhile contest. Few reputations were enhanced among the players, though one could admire the endeavour of scrum-half Andy Gregory, who had tried hard to find form when in Australia. In New Zealand Britain lost all three of the Tests for the first time. And they lost the third Test by the biggest winning score of any Kiwi team. How then was the tour other than a dismal failure?

The policy of the manager and the coach, from the day of their appointment, was to select a young squad. Skippered by the youngest-ever tour captain and with an average age of 24, the squad was made up of impressionable young men who were willing to learn. On tour, many watched club games, spoke to coaches and visited club training sessions when in Sydney and Brisbane. Ray Ashton and Des Foy, having seen a top Sydney club, Parramatta, in training, were stunned by the intensity and thought given to the club's training programme. While the British team had attained levels of fitness never before achieved, they found that this was accepted simply as normal abroad.

In both Australia and New Zealand, Britain proved that they do have players of genuine Test quality. Young Garry Schofield displayed a maturity far in advance of his years and showed true pace and positional sense. Des Drummond and Ellery Hanley drew praise from spectators wherever they played. Mick Burke was solid and dependable, especially when fielding high 'bombs', and centre Keith Mumby always stood his ground even when faced with players of greater pace. In the forwards, Andy Goodway revealed himself as the equal, Wayne Pearce apart, of any in the opposition ranks, being the only one powerful enough and fast enough to break the strongest tackles. Both hookers, Brian Noble and Kevin Beardmore, would grace any Test side, while the second-row forwards, Chris Burton and Mick Worrall, until injuries curtailed their activities, displayed glimpses of the hard work needed from modern forwards. But in the final analysis, the party as a whole was simply not good enough to sustain a tour of such length, and the weaknesses within the game in Britain were more than evident as the tour progressed.

At the luncheon held at Headingley, back in May, to announce the names of the tour squad, the media were glowing in their praise of the priority given to youth. Whatever differences of opinion existed with regard to individual selections, it was felt that a young, fit squad was needed to undertake such an arduous tour. But, with hindsight, the British party was too young and too inexperienced to cope with the pressures and stresses of twenty-four matches in thirteen weeks. Few British forwards could match the strength and physique of the Australian and New Zealand forwards, whose devotion to weight-training is certainly an advantage in meeting the demands of the modern game. Only Andy Goodway had the power to break tackles consistently, only he was able to make the 30-yard breaks so necessary to relieve pressure or to set up an attack. The British pack was also far too small. In one match they averaged 13 stone 10 pounds and 5 feet 10 inches in height. This lack of size, plus the fact that most of the forwards still tried to break the Australian and New Zealand defensive cover from the first-receiver position, meant that the Lions spent far too much time penned in their own half.

No British forward, save the hard working and experienced Mick Adams, could create play with his ball-handling skills and help to vary the often stereotyped tactics. Unfortunately, much of Adams's work was executed too slowly. Nor was there any player in the backs mature enough to act as pivot for midfield play; no one could assess the changing situation of a game, dictate the pattern of play, and create chances for the runners. Australia and New Zealand, on the other hand, had several such players. The loose forward and half-back combination is the dynamo of a team and here Britain were in trouble throughout the tour. It is impossible for a tour party to prepare for a Test series in Australia when, because of injuries or non-selection, the two half-backs for the crucial second and third Tests have completed only one full session of eighty minutes in the previous eleven games, but such was the case with Neil Holding and Tony Myler. Oldham's scrum-half, Ray Ashton, because of disc trouble, only completed three matches. And the true attacking skill of loose forward Harry Pinner and the endeavour of Terry Flanagan were available to the coach for only seven matches throughout Australia.

Despite their occasional attacking flair, one of the biggest problems faced by the Lions' backs was their inability to match the Australians in terms of physique. The British back division was a stone and a half lighter per man in all three of the Tests, a frightening deficiency, responsible for turning the advantage to Australia whenever they looked to be most vulnerable. The inability of Britain's backs to put Lewis, Miles, Grothe and Meninga to the floor in the tackle resulted in a crucial try which turned the game Australia's way in each Test. In the only worthwhile contest of the New Zealand Tests, it was the huge stand-off, Olsen Filipaina, who was to scatter Britain's defenders like ninepins, before setting up the tries for a Kiwi victory.

Unable to break the stranglehold defences of Australia and New Zealand, Britain rarely kicked well — only Burke and Hobbs, particularly in New Zealand, gaining the team any respite with their punts. Britain's kicks were often directed aimlessly upfield with few players following up to put pressure on the receiver. It is significant that Gary Jack, a controversial selection at full-back for Australia, was to become one of their successes, while Gary Kemble, the Kiwi full-back, was selected as the player-of-the-series in New Zealand. They could not have received more favourable treatment from Britain's kickers.

Though the deficiencies of the 1984 tour were not peculiar to any one section of the party, attitude and effort did fluctuate. In Australia the players gave their all, trained and worked harder than any British team I have known, and were proud and eager to achieve the rewards of their endeavours. That they did not was because there were simply too few players among them of genuine Test standard. By the time they arrived in Auckland, their 'all' had been given and was left across the Tasman Sea. A tour of two nations, as strong as Australia and New Zealand now are, is far too long, especially for a squad as young as this one. Their energy and motivation were sapped from the huge efforts made in Australia and many came to look on the latter half of the itinerary as light relief from the rigours of the earlier games. Many players' minds were already turned to thoughts of their eventual return home; a few were more interested in the accumulation of club T-shirts than Test caps. Frank Myler was probably right when he declared, 'We hit a high in Australia where we built up, and then felt an anti-climax. The edge has gone off us and we have not played well in New Zealand. We suffered a heavy toll in Australia with the result that our tackling has deteriorated rapidly.'

121

29 *and* 30.   Two of the Lions' squad who had an outstanding tour were Andy Goodway and Garry Schofield. Goodway (left) revealed himself as the equal of any in the opposition not only with the power to break tackles consistently but also to make the 30-yard breaks so

necessary to relieve pressure or to set up an attack. Garry Schofield (right), the youngest player in the touring party, displayed a maturity far in advance of his 18 years and showed true pace and remarkable positional sense in all the Tests in which he played.

The loss of Rod McKenzie, unable to accompany the Lions to New Zealand, removed the meticulous organization which had marked the Australian part of the tour. Forgetting rugby balls more than once for a training session, the inability to work a motivational cassette tape, the absence of any arrangements for taking tackle counts are comparatively small matters, but cumulatively they add up to a slackening of discipline. There is no point in criticizing the poor quality of the defence, which was torn to shreds by the bursts of the Sorenson brothers, Kevin Tamati, Hugh McGahan and Olsen Filipaina when at no time in the twenty-one days in New Zealand did Britain bring out the tackle shields at training.

There is little value in bemoaning the fact that Britain had only seventeen fit players from whom to choose the final Test team when the management had not been firm enough in assessing injury problems. Ron Barritt worked wonders to help the recovery of the players, but there was a limit to what even he could do. There was no excuse for encouraging a number of players to continue throughout the New Zealand tour when there was little hope of them getting fit. Some never played or completed only a single match. The continuing presence of the injured players, through no fault of their own, had a weakening and debilitating effect on the attitude of those still training, especially when one party trained hard in the rain while the other relaxed in the hotel swimming-pool. An injection of fresh players at the beginning of the New Zealand section of the tour would have provided the necessary boost to morale. If Rugby Union can fly a player out to play in one match, as happened on a recent tour, then surely the League, as professionals, should do the same for three Tests. In fairness, the Rugby Football League were prepared to do this but no call for replacements reached them.

Finally, there is little point in complaining that some players seemed not to want to play when neither manager nor coach was prepared to put the question: 'Do you want to play or do you want to fly home?' Such a question, posed on previous tours, should definitely have been put by a firm manager on this tour.

There is no doubt that morale did decline in New Zealand and team spirit ebbed. As results went against the touring party the inaction of an inevitably dispirited manager and coach caused the party to turn in on itself with the result that, in Christchurch and Auckland, for example, before the Tests, many players simply stayed isolated in their hotels. Their failure to attend luncheons and receptions, the lack of organised sightseeing tours to engender team spirit and to allow young players to relax together away from the pressures surrounding a Test match, all brought a sombre mood to the party in New Zealand.

All in all, apart from every aspect of Rod Mackenzie and Ron Barritt's work, the commitment of the players in Australia, the general level of results outside the Tests, and the healthy profits achieved by Roland Davis, who used all his expertise to bring in the money, there was actually not very much to enthuse about. It was a dull tour; there was little fun. Frank Myler, sometimes unsupported, did his best but, despite the sincerity and honesty of his approach, the task was beyond him, though I am sure that he, like many of us, only realized the immensity of the problems as the tour progressed. Now surely we must accept the 1984 tour as the last to embrace both Australia and New Zealand. Britain is not strong enough to mount another double tour, and the present strength and quality of New Zealand's play demands separate arrangements anyway. Whatever financial problems there may be, we should grasp the New Zealand chairman's offer to 'make it viable if Great Britain will make a separate tour in May and June'. Following the visits by New Zealand and Australia to Britain in 1985 and 1986, we should arrange two six-week tours, carrying less playing personnel, to New Zealand and Papua New Guinea in 1987 and to Australia in 1988. A four-yearly cycle of tours could then be maintained.

Any touring party is a pointer to the health of that nation's Rugby League, just as the teams who oppose it at Test level reflect the conditions abroad. The 1984 tour, perhaps more than any other, indicated the contrasting stages of development and the differing styles of play of all three nations. Australian players' standards of fitness and physique are awesome to behold. Their tactical planning, especially in relation to defensive strategies, is most impressive and they are always receptive to new ideas. Their national side is the end product of a fiercely competitive league system in Brisbane and Sydney, leagues which are continually fed with ambitious players from an endless number of country league teams.

Three victories in the Tests were surely the best advertisement for Rugby League in New Zealand, especially as the matches were shown live on television to an enthusiastic public. Though the club sides are weak in comparison to British sides and the game itself struggles in the wake of a publicity machine which seems to concentrate only on the All Blacks' Rugby Union side, the League game is nevertheless making great strides forward – thanks to a successful national team. New Zealand is the perfect example of a fine national side dragging the game out of the backwoods and setting it before an enthusiastic public. With increased media coverage and more sponsorship, the game must thrive. But what of Great Britain?

The past eighteen months have not been entirely wasted for at least the Rugby Football League has a new administrative structure from which perhaps a successful side can be helped to grow. But if the new nine-man management committee also fails, it should be scrapped, along with the Rugby League council, and the task handed over to the paid officials of the game, free of club affiliations. Ken Arthurson, Ron McAuliffe and Ron McGregor, the respective chairmen of the New South Wales, Queensland and New Zealand Rugby Leagues, are not bound by thirty-man councils. They are powerful autocrats, working with a small band of paid officials for the good of the game. Without first-class international competition a sport stagnates, and there is no doubt that Britain's recent failures at international level are a direct result of weaknesses in the structure of the game in this country.

On the other hand, there is real hope for the future in the success of the National Coaching Scheme. If Phil Larder is given his head, with added strength from the recent influx of first-class Australian players whose presence has helped to transform training sessions at many of the British clubs they have joined; if a streamlined executive committee can bring new disciplines to management; if the casual approach of too many players and coaches can be eradicated; and if the money now coming into Rugby League through sponsorship and imaginative marketing can be invested wisely in the development of the game, especially in schools and at youth level, then I remain confident about the long-term future of British Rugby League.

Appendix 1

THE LIONS IN AUSTRALIA

Richardson Park, Darwin, 18 May: Northern Territory 13 Great Britain 40

Northern Territory: Doyle (Alice Springs); Given (Darwin), Masterson (Darwin), Smith (Darwin), Abion (Darwin); Larder (Darwin), Harrison (Darwin); Blackburn (Darwin), McGuire (Darwin), Simmonds (Darwin), Jaeger (Gove), Lumby (Alice Springs), Brown (Darwin)

Substitutes: Ryan (Darwin), Brown (Darwin), Adler (Darwin), Wilson (Alice Springs) not used

Scorers: try – Larder; goals – Doyle (4); drop goal – Doyle

Great Britain: Mumby; Drummond, Duane, Hanley, Foy; Donlan, Ashton; Rayne, Noble, Goodway, Worrall, Hobbs, Pinner

Substitutes: Joyner for Duane after 9 minutes, Crooks for Hobbs after 54 minutes, Holding for Ashton after 54 minutes, Flanagan not used

Scorers: tries – Noble (2), Goodway (2), Hanley, Drummond, Donlan, Foy; goals – Crooks (3), Hobbs

Referee: D. Carey

Attendance: 7,286

Appendix 1

Eric Weissel Oval, Wagga Wagga, 23 May: Riverina 18 Great Britain 22

Riverina: Maguire (Batlow); Dennis (Gundagai), Rawiri (Cootamundra), Sellars (Tumut), Rosetto (Griffith Waratah); Trudgett (Yenda), Ward (Gundagai); Hogan (Narrandera), Morgan (Yanco Wamoon), Lewis (Weethalle), Scarfone (Griffith B/W), Stockton (Wagga Magpies), Pilon (West Wyalong)

Substitutes: Lyons (Gundagai), Pryce (West Kangaroos) not used

Scorers: tries – Dennis, Ward, Rawiri; goals – Dennis (3)

Great Britain: Burke; Clarke, Lydon, Hanley, Schofield; Smith, Gregory; Case, Beardmore, Crooks, Flanagan, Goodway, Adams

Substitutes: Holding for Gregory after 60 minutes, Burton for Flanagan after 67 minutes, Proctor and Donlan not used

Scorers: tries – Lydon, Burke, Holding; goals – Burke (5)

Referee: B. Foran

Attendance: 3,716

Wauchope, 25 May: North Coast 6 Great Britain 56

North Coast: Mulvaney; Buckley, Cordner, Knight, Davis; Robert Laurie, Hinton; Walsh, Key, Warwick, Corfe, Hurrell, Anderson

Substitutes: Foley for Walsh after 44 minutes, Richard Laurie for Mulvaney after 54 minutes, Kelley not used

Scorers: try – Key; goal – Cordner

Great Britain: Mumby; Drummond, Lydon, Joyner, Clark; Donlan, Holding; Rayne, Noble, O'Neill, Proctor, Worrall, Adams

Substitutes: Ashton for Holding after 40 minutes, Hobbs for Adams after 40 minutes, Burton for Proctor after 58 minutes

Scorers: tries – Drummond (3), Clark (2), Lydon (2), Noble, Holding, Proctor; goals – Lydon (8)

Referee: B. Sullivan

Attendance: 4,200

Australia

Victoria Park, Dubbo, 27 May: Western Division 30   Great Britain 36

Western Division: Gordon; Haynes, Smith, Spurr, Williams; McWhirter, Douglas; Horton, Jayett, Miller, Wright, McPhail, Jackson

Substitutes: Moy, Fisher not used

Scorers: tries – Smith, McWhirter, Haynes, Douglas; goals – Jayett (7)

Great Britain: Burke; Drummond, Lydon, Mumby, Foy; Myler, Ashton; Rayne, Noble, Crooks, Burton, Goodway, Pinner

Substitutes: Schofield for Myler after 57 minutes, Hobbs for Pinner after 57 minutes, Holding and Proctor not used

Scorers: tries – Foy (3), Crooks, Ashton, Noble, Mumby; goals – Burke (4)

Referee: L. Harrigan

Attendance: 4,528

Sydney Cricket Ground, Sydney, 30 May: North Sydney 8   Great Britain 14

North Sydney: Portlock; Sheppard, Tait, Brockwell, Simons; Lonergan, Spina; Jennings, Cross, Cooper, McKinnon, Ritchie, Johnston

Substitutes: Luckman for Sheppard after 32 minutes, Hillier for Johnston after 58 minutes, Casey for Portlock after 62 minutes

Scorers: tries – Luckman, Simons

Great Britain: Burke; Drummond, Schofield, Mumby, Foy; Donlan, Gregory; Rayne, Beardmore, Crooks, Goodway, Burton, Adams

Substitutes: Worrall for Crooks after 30 minutes, Case for Rayne after 61 minutes, Holding and Smith not used

Scorers: tries – Drummond, Goodway; goals – Burke (3)

Referee: B. Barnes

Attendance: 4,067

International Sports Centre, Newcastle, 2 June: Newcastle 18 Great Britain 28

Newcastle: Elwin (Western Suburbs); Bates (North Newcastle), Connor (Lakes United), Dedman (Western Suburbs), Murray (Western Suburbs); Eagar (North Newcastle), Higgins (North Newcastle); Martine (Western Suburbs), Pitman (Kurri Kurri), Graham (Western Suburbs), Farrar (Western Suburbs), Wright (North Newcastle), Burrows (Maitland)

Substitutes: Taylor (Lakes United) for Higgins after 40 minutes

Scorers: tries – Higgins, Martine; goals – Elwin (5)

Great Britain: Burke; Clark, Hanley, Smith, Basnett; Schofield, Holding; O'Neill, Noble, Crooks, Hobbs, Worrall, Flanagan

Substitutes: Pinner for Crooks after 40 minutes, Lydon for Smith after 51 minutes

Scorers: tries – Schofield, Flanagan, Hanley, Holding, Clark; goals – Burke (4)

Referee: B. Priest

Attendance: 11,500

Sydney Cricket Ground, 9 June: Australia 25 Great Britain 8

Australia: Jack (Balmain, Sydney); Boustead (Manly, Sydney), Miles (Wynnum-Manly, Brisbane), Kenny (Parramatta, Sydney), Conlon (Canterbury-Bankstown, Sydney); Lewis (Wynnum-Manly, Brisbane) captain, Murray (Redcliffe, Brisbane); Brown (Manly, Sydney), Conescu (Gladstone, Brisbane), Dowling (Wynnum-Manly, Brisbane), Pearce (Balmain, Sydney), Niebling (Redcliffe, Brisbane), Price (Parramatta, Sydney)

Substitutes: Young (St George, Sydney) for Brown after 68 minutes, Close (Manly, Sydney) not used

Scorers: tries – Lewis, Boustead, Murray; goals – Conlon (4); drop goal – Lewis

Great Britain: Burke (Widnes); Drummond (Leigh), Schofield (Hull), Mumby (Bradford Northern), Hanley (Bradford Northern); Foy (Oldham), Holding (St Helens); Crooks (Hull), Noble (Bradford Northern) captain, Goodway (Oldham), Burton (Hull KR), Worrall (Oldham), Adams (Widnes)

Substitutes: Lydon (Widnes) for Holding after 23 minutes, Hobbs (Featherstone Rovers) for Crooks after 72 minutes

Scorers: try – Schofield; goals – Burke (2)

Referee: R. Shrimpton (New Zealand)

Attendance: 30,190

Salter Oval, Bundaberg, 11 June: Wide Bay 18   Great Britain 28

Wide Bay: Birmingham; Kiss, Gorman, Curran, King; Browning, Ovens; Slater, Berkery, Harch, Molyneux, Gerrard, McDougall

Substitutes: Glaxier for Birmingham after 56 minutes, Dansey for Gerrard after 59 minutes

Scorers: tries – Gorman, Ovens, Slater; goals – Birmingham (2), Kiss

Great Britain: Lydon; Clark, Smith, Hanley, Basnett; Joyner, Gregory; O'Neill, Beardmore, Case, Proctor, Flanagan, Pinner

Substitutes: Myler for Hanley after 40 minutes, Worrall for Pinner after 65 minutes

Scorers: tries – Hanley, Proctor, Beardmore, Basnett, Worrall; goals – Lydon (4)

Referee: M. Hourigan

Attendance: 2,316

Browne Park, Rockhampton, 15 June: Central Queensland 12 Great Britain 44

Central Queensland: Tuppea (Central Highlands); McLaughlin (Rockhampton), McDonald (Callide Valley), Miller (Rockhampton), Curran (Gladstone); Jenson (Gladstone), Hunt (Callide Valley); Brazier (Rockhampton), Anderson (Callide Valley), George (Callide Valley), Blackadder (Gladstone), Taylor (Gladstone), Day (Callide Valley)

Substitutes: Golden for McDonald after 57 minutes, Hanson not used

Scorers: tries – Anderson, Curran; goals – McDonald (2)

Great Britain: Burke; Drummond, Schofield, Mumby, Hanley; Myler, Gregory; Rayne, Noble, Goodway, Proctor, Burton, Worrall

Substitutes: Ashton for Gregory after 40 minutes, Adams for Worrall after 40 minutes

Scorers: tries – Schofield (4), Mumby, Drummond, Proctor (2); goals – Burke, Schofield (5)

Referee: L. McCosh   Attendance: 5,371

Townsville, 17 June: Northern Queensland 20 Great Britain 38

Northern Queensland: Brunker; Foran, Deemal, Gengilley, Shearer; Duncan, Price; Bocos, Morrissey, Bleakney, Colwell, Smith, Baker

Substitutes: Barclay for Brunker after 33 minutes, Keogh for Shearer after 57 minutes

Scorers: tries – Colwell, Foran, Morrissey, Barclay; goals – Smith (2)

Great Britain: Lydon; Drummond, Hanley, Smith, Basnett; Joyner, Ashton; Crooks, Beardmore, Case, O'Neill, Proctor, Pinner

Substitutes: Adams for Crooks after 65 minutes, Foy for Hanley after 67 minutes

Scorers: tries – Hanley (2), Drummond (2), Beardmore, Smith, Basnett; goals – Lydon (5)

Referee: B. Gomersall   Attendance: 6,036

Athletic Oval, Toowoomba, 20 June: Toowoomba 18   Great Britain 16

Toowoomba: Gill; Gibson, Milne, Coutts, Tynan; Tew, Smith; Stains, Hanna, Hohn, McCullough, Fitzgerald, McKinnon

Substitutes: Smith for McKinnon after 59 minutes, Reis for Milne after 66 minutes

Scorers: tries – Coutts, Stains, Gibson; goals – Coutts (3)

Great Britain: Donlan; Clarke, Smith, Foy, Basnett; Joyner, Gregory; O'Neill, Beardmore, Case, Proctor, Hobbs, Pinner

Substitutes: Ashton for Foy after 23 minutes, Adams for Joyner after 59 minutes

Scorers: tries – Basnett, Clarke, Smith; goals – Hobbs (2)

Referee: G. Giebels   Attendance: 4,051

Lang Park, Brisbane, 26 June: Australia 18   Great Britain 6

Australia: Jack (Balmain, Sydney); Grothe (Parramatta, Sydney), Miles (Wynnum-Manly, Brisbane), Meninga (Souths, Brisbane), Boustead (Manly, Sydney); Lewis (Wynnum-Manly, Brisbane) captain, Murray (Redcliffe, Brisbane); Brown (Manly, Sydney), Conescu (Gladstone, Brisbane), Dowling (Wynnum-Manly, Brisbane), Vautin (Manly, Sydney), Niebling (Redcliffe, Brisbane), Pearce (Balmain, Sydney)

Substitutes: Fullerton-Smith (Redcliffe, Brisbane) for Brown after 66 minutes, Mortimer (Canterbury-Bankstown, Sydney) not used

Scorers: tries – Grothe, Pearce, Meninga; goals – Meninga (3)

Great Britain: Burke (Widnes); Drummond (Leigh), Schofield (Hull), Mumby (Bradford Northern), Hanley (Bradford Northern); Myler (Widnes), Holding (St Helens); Rayne (Leeds), Noble (Bradford Northern) captain, Crooks (Hull), Burton (Hull KR), Goodway (Oldham), Worrall (Oldham)

Substitutes: Adams (Widnes) for Crooks after 18 minutes, Gregory (Widnes) for Burke after 71 minutes

Scorers: try – Schofield; goal – Burke

Referee: R. Shrimpton (New Zealand)   Attendance: 26,534

Tweed Heads, 28 June: Northern Rivers 12   Great Britain 24

Northern Rivers: O'Neill (Seagulls); Miles (Ballina), Ryan (Seagulls), Howie (Old Boys), O'Neill (Cudgen); Hughes (Lismore Marist Brothers), Kennedy (Casino); Miles (Ballina), Dorrough (Seagulls), Brokenshire (Mururl-lumbah Brothers), Judd (Seagulls), Clarke (Casino), Ferris (Cudgen)

Substitutes: Garland (Bibambil) for Brokenshire after 16 minutes, Hall (Seagulls) for O'Neill after 36 minutes, Plummer (Lower Clarence) for Kennedy after 49 minutes

Scorers: tries – O'Neill (2); goals – Hughes, Hall

Great Britain: Lydon; Drummond, Schofield, Smith, Clarke; Donlan, Gregory; O'Neill, Beardmore, Case, Proctor, Hobbs, Pinner

Substitutes: Foy for Schofield after 22 minutes, Worrall for O'Neill after 63 minutes, Basnett not used

Scorers: tries – Clarke, Drummond, Hobbs, Smith; goals – Lydon (2), Hobbs (2)

Referee: S. Asbury

Attendance: 3,537

Scully Park, Tamworth, 1 July: Northern Division, NSW 18   Great Britain 32

Northern Division, NSW: Donnelly; Archdale, McCann, Lennan, Brady; Hill, R. McCormack; G. McCormack, Carr, Thompson, Whittaker, Frazer, Hayward

Substitutes: Earl for Whittaker after 40 minutes, Craigie for R. McCormack after 40 minutes, McKinnon for McCann after 52 minutes, Butters for Hayward after 52 minutes

Scorers: tries – Carr, Donnelly, Hill; goals – Donnelly (3)

Great Britain: Lydon; Drummond, Hanley, Smith, Clark; Myler, Ashton; Rayne, Beardmore, Case, Hobbs, O'Neill, Adams

Substitutes: Holding for Myler after 68 minutes, Proctor for Rayne after 71 minutes

Scorers: tries – Hanley (2), Lydon, Smith, Case; goals – Lydon (6)

Referee: N. Hockey

Attendance: 6,750

Sydney Cricket Ground, 7 July: Australia 20   Great Britain 7

Australia: Jack (Balmain, Sydney); Grothe (Parramatta, Sydney), Miles (Wynnum-Manly, Brisbane), Meninga (Souths, Brisbane), Boustead (Manly, Sydney); Lewis (Wynnum-Manly, Brisbane) captain, Mortimer (Canterbury-Bankstown, Sydney); Niebling (Redcliffe, Brisbane), Conescu (Gladstone, Brisbane), Dowling (Wynnum-Manly, Brisbane), Fullerton-Smith (Redcliffe, Brisbane), Pearce (Balmain, Sydney), Price (Parramatta, Sydney)

Substitutes: Brown (Manly, Sydney) for Fullerton-Smith after 62 minutes, Kenny (Parramatta, Sydney) for Miles after 68 minutes

Scorers: tries – Grothe, Conescu, Jack; goals – Meninga (4)

Great Britain: Burke (Widnes); Drummond (Leigh), Schofield (Hull), Mumby (Bradford Northern), Hanley (Bradford Northern); Myler (Widnes), Holding (St Helens); Case (Wigan), Noble (Bradford Northern) captain, Hobbs (Featherstone Rovers), Burton (Hull KR), Goodway (Oldham), Adams (Widnes)

Substitutes: Smith (Hull KR), Rayne (Leeds) not used

Scorers: try – Hanley; goal – Burke; drop goal – Holding

Referee: T. Drake (New Zealand)

Attendance: 18,756

THE LIONS IN NEW ZEALAND
AND PAPUA NEW GUINEA

Jubilee Park, Whangarei, 10 July:
Northern Districts 8   Great Britain 42

Northern Districts: Huruwai; Horo, Baker, Rapana, Curtis; Stewart, Ramsay; Poasa, Pirichi, Toa, Thomas, Smeath, Campbell

Substitutes: Donaldson for Ramsay after 64 minutes, Horo for Campbell after 70 minutes

Scorers: tries – Smeath, Campbell

Great Britain: Mumby; Clark, Smith, Joyner, Basnett; Donlan, Gregory; Hobbs, Beardmore, Rayne, Proctor, O'Neill, Adams

Substitutes: Schofield for Mumby after 45 minutes, Case for Hobbs after 79 minutes

Scorers: tries – Basnett, Proctor, Adams, Beardmore, Clark, Gregory, Joyner, Smith; goals – Hobbs (4), Schofield

Referee: K. Bailey

Attendance: 1,600

Carlaw Park, Auckland, 14 July: New Zealand 12   Great Britain 0

New Zealand: Kemble (Auckland & Hull); O'Hara (Auckland & Hull), Leuluai (Auckland & Hull), Ah Kuoi (Auckland & Hull) captain, Bell (Auckland & Leeds); Filipaina (Balmain, Sydney), Varley (Auckland & Leigh); Kevin Tamati (Wellington & Widnes), Howie Tamati (Taranaki & Wigan), Dane Sorenson (Eastern Suburbs, Sydney), Kurt Sorenson (Eastern Suburbs, Sydney), Wright (Auckland), McGahan (Auckland)

Substitutes: Friend (Auckland) for Filipaina after 78 minutes, Cowan (Auckland) not used

Scorers: tries – Leuluai, Ah Kuoi; goals – Filipaina (2)

Great Britain: Burke (Widnes); Drummond (Leigh), Schofield (Hull), Mumby (Bradford Northern), Hanley (Bradford Northern); Smith (Hull KR), Holding (St Helens); Hobbs (Featherstone Rovers), Noble (Bradford Northern) captain, Case (Wigan), Goodway (Oldham), Burton (Hull KR), Adams (Widnes)

Substitutes: Gregory (Widnes), Joyner (Castleford) not used

Referee: K. Roberts (Australia)   Attendance: 8,500

Davies Park, Huntly, 15 July: Maoris 8   Great Britain 19

Maoris: Wright (Auckland); Uluave (Manawatu), Lovett (Auckland), Ropati (Auckland), Kupa (Wellington); O'Regan (Auckland), Katene (Wellington); Poasa (Northland), McGregor (Auckland), Murray (Northland), Tuuta (Canterbury), Muller (Auckland), Pine (Taranaki)

Substitutes: Clarke (Waikato) for Poasa after 53 minutes, Waitai (Auckland) for Tuuta after 72 minutes

Scorers: try – Uluave; goals – Wright (2)

Great Britain: Mumby; Drummond, Lydon, Foy, Basnett; Joyner, Gregory; Rayne, Beardmore, Crooks, Proctor, O'Neill, Flanagan

Substitutes: Hanley for Lydon after 20 minutes, Burton for Crooks after 25 minutes

Scorers: tries – Foy, Flanagan, Beardmore; goals – Hanley (3); drop goal – Gregory

Referee: K. Blackler   Attendance: 2,397

Hutt Recreation Field, Wellington, 18 July:
Central Districts 6   Great Britain 38

Central Districts: Miritana; Lajpold, Kupa, Rutene, Tangira; Pupuke, Katene; Pine, Harvey, Henry, Kuiti, Stewart, Rasmussen

Substitutes: Uluare for Pupuke after 40 minutes, Jackson for Pine after 61 minutes

Scorers: try – Rasmussen; goal – Miritana

Great Britain: Burke; Clark, Donlan, Smith, Basnett; Myler, Gregory; Rayne, Noble, O'Neill, Flanagan, Case, Joyner

Substitutes: Lydon for Myler after 40 minutes, Adams not used

Scorers: tries – Noble (2), Smith, Gregory (2), Clark, Donlan; goals – Burke (4), Lydon

Referee: D. Wilson

Attendance: 2,061

Addington Showgrounds, Christchurch, 22 July:
New Zealand 28   Great Britain 12

New Zealand: Kemble (Auckland & Hull); O'Hara (Auckland & Hull), Leuluai (Auckland & Hull), Ah Kuoi (Auckland & Hull) captain, Bell (Auckland & Leeds); Filipaina (Balmain, Sydney), Varley (Auckland & Leigh); Kevin Tamati (Wellington & Widnes), Howie Tamati (Taranaki & Wigan), Dane Sorenson (Eastern Suburbs, Sydney), Kurt Sorenson (Eastern Suburbs, Sydney), Wright (Auckland), McGahan (Auckland)

Substitutes: Friend (Auckland) for Varley after 73 minutes, Cowan (Auckland) for Howie Tamati after 73 minutes

Scorers: tries – O'Hara (2), Bell, Leuluai, Ah Kuoi; goals – Filipaina (4)

Great Britain: Burke (Widnes); Drummond (Leigh), Hanley (Bradford Northern), Mumby (Bradford Northern), Lydon (Widnes); Myler (Widnes), Gregory (Widnes); Hobbs (Featherstone Rovers), Noble (Bradford Northern) captain, Case (Wigan), Goodway (Oldham), Burton (Hull KR), Adams (Widnes)

Substitutes: Joyner (Castleford) for Burton after 45 minutes, Beardmore (Castleford) for Noble after 64 minutes

Scorers: tries – Myler, Hanley; goals – Burke (2)

Referee: B. Barnes (Australia)

Attendance: 3,800

Addington Showgrounds, Christchurch, 25 July:
South Island 14   Great Britain 36

South Island: Alfeld; Crequer, Kilkelly, McDonald, Moi Moi; Field, Gibb; Dwyer, Wallace, Taylor, Barrow, Tuuta, Edkins

Substitutes: Shelford for Tuuta after 50 minutes, Forsey for Gibb after 66 minutes

Scorers: tries – Gibb (2); goals – Edkins (3)

Great Britain: Mumby; Clark, Hanley, Joyner, Basnett; Donlan, Holding; Crooks, Beardmore, Hobbs, Burton, O'Neill, Flanagan

Substitutes: Adams for Crooks after 40 minutes, Burke for Beardmore after 66 minutes

Scorers: tries – Beardmore (3), Basnett (2), Mumby, Hanley; goals – Hobbs (4)

Referee: T. Drake

Attendance: 2,500

Carlaw Park, Auckland, 28 July: New Zealand 32   Great Britain 16

New Zealand: Kemble (Auckland & Hull); O'Hara (Auckland & Hull), Leuluai (Auckland & Hull), Ah Kuoi (Auckland & Hull) captain, Bell (Auckland & Leeds); Filipaina (Balmain, Sydney), Varley (Auckland & Leigh); Kevin Tamati (Wellington & Widnes), Howie Tamati (Taranaki & Wigan), Dane Sorenson (Eastern Suburbs, Sydney), Kurt Sorenson (Eastern Suburbs, Sydney), Wright (Auckland), McGahan (Auckland)

Substitutes: Friend (Auckland) for Varley after 52 minutes, Cowan (Auckland) for McGahan after 71 minutes

Scorers: tries – O'Hara, Leuluai (2), Friend (2); goals – Filipaina (6)

Great Britain: Burke (Widnes); Drummond (Leigh), Hanley (Bradford Northern), Mumby (Bradford Northern), Lydon (Widnes); Myler (Widnes), Gregory (Widnes); Hobbs (Featherstone Rovers), Noble (Bradford Northern) captain, Case (Wigan), Adams (Widnes), Goodway (Oldham), Flanagan (Oldham)

Substitutes: Joyner (Castleford) for Case after 58 minutes, Donlan (Leigh) for Burke after 71 minutes

Scorers: tries – Mumby, Hanley; goals – Burke (4)

Referee: K. Roberts (Australia)   Attendance: 7,500

Carlaw Park, Auckland, 31 July: Auckland 18   Great Britain 16

Auckland: Williams; Lovett, Bell, O'Regan, Ropati; Cooper, Friend; Cowan, Hooker, Kevin Tamati, Howells, Ackland, Wright

Substitutes: Swart, Ah Kuoi not used

Scorers: tries – Cooper (2), Lovett; goals – Lovett (3)

Great Britain: Burke; Drummond, Hanley, Mumby, Basnett; Donlan, Gregory; Rayne, Noble, Goodway, Hobbs, Proctor, Flanagan

Substitutes: Smith for Burke after 64 minutes, Adams not used

Scorers: tries – Goodway (2), Proctor; goals – Hobbs (2)

Referee: R. Shrimpton   Attendance: 6,100

The Lions in Papua New Guinea

Mount Hagen, 5 August: Papua New Guinea 20   Great Britain 38

Papua New Guinea: Kitimun; Karai, Noifa, Numapo, Tolik; Gabob, Kila; Tep captain, Asarufa, Jekis, Kubak, Loitive, Taumaku

Substitutes: Peter for Kila after 40 minutes, Wek for Loitive after 68 minutes

Scorers: tries – Tolik, Noifa, Jekis, Taumaku; goals – Numapo (2)

Great Britain: Burke (Widnes); Drummond (Leigh), Hanley (Bradford Northern), Mumby (Bradford Northern), Lydon (Widnes); Myler (Widnes), Gregory (Widnes); Rayne (Leeds), Noble (Bradford Northern) captain, Goodway (Oldham), Flanagan (Oldham), Hobbs (Featherstone Rovers), Adams (Widnes)

Substitutes: Donlan for Myler after 10 minutes, Proctor for Lydon after 40 minutes

Scorers: tries – Dummond (2), Burke, Mumby, Rayne, Hanley, Hobbs; goals – Burke (5)

Referee: B. Gomersall (Australia)

Attendance: 7,510

Appendix 3

APPEARANCES AND SCORERS

	Appearances (as substitute in brackets)		Scorers	
	In Tests	*In other matches*	*Tries*	*Goals*
Adams	6 (+1)	5 (+4)	1	–
Ashton	–	4 (+3)	1	–
Basnett	–	9	6	–
Beardmore	– (+1)	10	7	–
Burke	7	7 (+1)	2	36
Burton	5	4 (+3)	–	–
Case	4	8 (+1)	1	–
Clark	–	10	7	–
Crooks	2	7 (+1)	1	3
Donlan	– (+2)	9	2	–
Drummond	7	10	11	–
Duane	–	1	–	–
Flanagan	2	7	2	–
Foy	1	5 (+2)	5	–
Goodway	7	6	5	–
Gregory	3 (+1)	9 (+1)	3	1 drop goal

| | Appearances (as substitute in brackets) | | Scorers | |
	In Tests	*In other matches*	*Tries*	*Goals*
Hanley	7	9 (+1)	12	3
Hobbs	5 (+1)	7 (+3)	2	15
Holding	4	3 (+4)	3	1 drop goal
Joyner	– (+2)	8 (+1)	1	–
Lydon	3 (+1)	8 (+2)	4	26
Mumby	7	9	5	–
Myler	5	4 (+1)	1	–
Noble (captain)	7	7	6	–
O'Neill	–	11	–	–
Pinner	–	6 (+1)	–	–
Proctor	– (+1)	9 (+1)	6	–
Rayne	2	11	1	–
Schofield	4	5 (+2)	7	6
Smith	1	9 (+2)	6	–
Worrall	2	4 (+3)	1	–

The publication of this book was made possible
through the generosity of Modern Maintenance Products,
Harrogate, Yorkshire.